*Charles Dickens*

# VIP
*Very Interesting People*

*Bite-sized biographies of Britain's most
fascinating historical figures*

CURRENTLY AVAILABLE

FORTHCOMING

# Charles Dickens

*VIP*
*Very Interesting People*

Michael Slater

OXFORD
UNIVERSITY PRESS

# OXFORD
**UNIVERSITY PRESS**

Great Clarendon Street, Oxford ox2 6DP

Oxford University Press is a department of the University of Oxford.
It furthers the University's objective of excellence in research, scholarship,
and education by publishing worldwide in

Oxford New York

Auckland Cape Town Dar es Salaam Hong Kong Karachi
Kuala Lumpur Madrid Melbourne Mexico City Nairobi
New Delhi Shanghai Taipei Toronto

With offices in

Argentina Austria Brazil Chile Czech Republic France Greece
Guatemala Hungary Italy Japan Poland Portugal Singapore
South Korea Switzerland Thailand Turkey Ukraine Vietnam

Oxford is a registered trade mark of Oxford University Press
in the UK and in certain other countries

Published in the United States
by Oxford University Press Inc., New York

First published in the *Oxford Dictionary of National Biography* 2004
This paperback edition first published 2007

British Library Cataloguing in Publication Data
Data available

Library of Congress Cataloging in Publication Data
Data available

Typeset by SPI Publisher Services, Pondicherry, India
Printed in Great Britain
on acid-free paper by
Ashford Colour Press Ltd., Gosport, Hants.

ISBN 978–0–19–921352–8 (Pbk.)

10 9 8 7 6 5 4 3 2 1

# Contents

# *Preface*

'The chief difficulty which faced Forster', wrote K. J. Fielding, referring to the first major biography of Dickens written by his intimate friend John Forster, 'was the one which confronts all Dickens biographers, and that is the enormous scope and variety of Dickens's career: every day of his life was packed with activity and incident, and almost everything he wrote cried out for quotation' (*Charles Dickens*, British Council 'Writers and Their Work' series, 1960). This difficulty is, of course, greatly intensified when the attempt is made, as it is here, to tell the story of Dickens's life within strict limits as to space. In this study, written originally for the *Oxford Dictionary of National Biography*, I have tried to meet it by focusing primarily (after a short account of Dickens's childhood, youth and early manhood) upon what Forster singled out as being of prime importance, 'the story of his books...at all stages of their progress'. Thus the emphasis of this short life falls upon Dickens's career as a phenomenally productive and phenomenally popular writer, both of fiction and non-fiction, while as much attention as possible is also paid to the main events in his personal life, such as his very public separation from his wife in 1858, as well as to his crowded and richly-documented social life, his astoundingly extensive and unremitting charitable activities, and his hugely successful second career as a public reader of his own works.

The 'Dickens industry', as it is sometimes called, continues at full throttle. New books and numerous scholarly articles devoted to him and his work are published every year. Among more recent publications have been a new biography by Jane Smiley (*Charles Dickens*, 2002), and a book that extends and deepens our knowledge of Dickens the writer in a hitherto little-explored area of his literary output, *Dickens the Journalist* by John Drew (2003). The magnificent British Academy Pilgrim Edition of Dickens's letters ended with volume 12 (2002) but new letters continue to surface regularly and are published in successive Supplements to Pilgrim in *The Dickensian*.

At the end of this short life I offer a brief survey of Dickens's after-fame including some account of the history of the exploitation of his work by the theatre, cinema, radio and television. This is something that also continues in full force, a particularly notable recent example of such media interest in Dickens being Andrew Davies's ground-breaking 2005 adaptation of *Bleak House* in fifteen half-hour episodes, shown in prime time on BBC1 television, immediately following a popular soap opera. This modern equivalent of Dickens's original publication of his novels in monthly or weekly instalments proved hugely popular, providing impressive testimony to the continuing power of Dickens's ability to attract and hold a mass audience.

*Michael Slater*
*September 2006*

## *About the author*

Michael Slater is Emeritus Professor of Victorian Literature at Birkbeck College, University of London, and a former Editor of *The Dickensian*. He is author of *Dickens and Women* (1983), and editor, with John Drew, of the Dent Uniform Edition of Dickens's Journalism (1994–2000). He is currently writing a major new biography of Dickens for Yale University Press.

# The making of a writer

*1*

*Charles John Huffam Dickens*
(1812–1870), novelist, was born on 7 February 1812
at 13 Mile End Terrace, Portsea, Portsmouth (since
1903 the Dickens Birthplace Museum), the second
child and first son of John Dickens (1785–1851),
an assistant clerk in the navy pay office, stationed
since 1808 in Portsmouth as an 'outport' worker,
and his wife, Elizabeth, *née* Barrow (1789–1863).

## Parents and siblings

Dickens's father, John, was the younger son of
William Dickens (*d*. 1785) and Elizabeth Ball
(*d*. 1824), respectively butler and housekeeper
in the Crewe family, who had married in 1781.
Old Mrs Dickens was fondly remembered by
the Crewe children as 'an inimitable story-teller'

(Allen, 12). On 13 June 1809 John married Elizabeth Barrow; her father, Charles Barrow, was a senior official in the navy pay office who shortly afterwards had to flee the country, having been detected embezzling public money. John's genial and convivial personality, his air of gentility, his financial improvidence, and his fondness for grandiloquent phrases are all mirrored in Mr Micawber in *David Copperfield*. Certain of these traits reappear in the character of Mr Dorrit (*Little Dorrit*) where, however, they are presented much less sympathetically. Elizabeth seems to have had, like her husband, a lively and irrepressibly optimistic temperament and aspects of her personality have traditionally been identified in both Mrs Nickleby (*Nicholas Nickleby*) and Mrs Micawber.

The couple's first child, the musically talented Frances Dickens, always known as Fanny, was born in 1810 and was a much loved companion during Dickens's earliest years. In 1837 she married the singer Henry Burnett (1811–1893) and remained very dear to Dickens until her untimely death from consumption in 1848; he commemorated their childhood companionship in his journal *Household Words* (6 April

1850) with a piece entitled 'A Child's Dream of a Star' (*Reprinted Pieces*, 1858). John's and Elizabeth's other children, born after Charles, were: Alfred Allen, who died in infancy in 1814; Letitia Mary (1816–1893), who married the architect, civil engineer, and active sanitary reformer Henry Austin; Harriet, born in 1819, who died in childhood; Frederick William, always known as Fred (1820–1868); Alfred Lamert (1822–1860); and Augustus Newnham (1827–1866). Alfred Lamert was the only one of Dickens's brothers to make a satisfactory career for himself (as a civil engineer); in adult life the marital problems and generally feckless behaviour of both Fred and Augustus created annoyances for Dickens (as did the continued financial irresponsibility of his father) but he seems always to have retained some brotherly affection for them—even for Augustus, who in 1857 deserted his blind wife and emigrated with another woman to Chicago, living openly with her there as 'Mr and Mrs Dickens'.

## Childhood and education

After a two-year spell back in London working in Somerset House (1815–16), John Dickens was posted first, briefly, to Sheerness and then to Chatham, where he settled with his growing family at 2 Ordnance Terrace, a six-roomed house, advertised as 'commanding beautiful views ... and fit for the residence of a genteel family' (Allen, 40). His income was rising but so were expenses. Two live-in servants were employed, one of whom, the teenage nursemaid Mary Weller, later gave Robert Langton her reminiscences of Dickens as a child. Dickens recalled his mother teaching him, 'thoroughly well', the alphabet and the rudiments of English and, later, Latin (Forster, 4). He and Fanny attended a nearby dame-school and later (1821?–1822?) he became a promising pupil at a 'classical, mathematical, and commercial school' run by the Revd William Giles, the son of a Baptist minister.

By now the family had moved into a slightly smaller house, 18 St Mary's Place, perhaps as a result of John Dickens's increasing financial diffi-culties. These Chatham years were hugely impor-tant for the development of Dickens's imagina-tion. His vivid, astonishingly detailed, memories of everything he experienced there, and of his voracious childhood reading (he was, Mary Weller recalled, 'a terrible boy to read'; Langton, 25), richly fed his later fiction and inspired some of his finest journalistic essays. Being 'a very little and a very sickly boy ... subject to attacks of violent spasm' (Forster, 3), he was debarred from sporting activities, though he enjoyed games of make-believe with his friends and getting up magic-lantern shows, also performing (sometimes as duets with Fanny) comic songs and recitations with, according to Mary Weller, '*such* action and *such* attitudes' (Langton, 26). John Dickens was proud of his children's singing talents which were sometimes publicly exhibited at the Mitre tavern in Rochester. This old city, which adjoins Chatham, with its ruined castle, ancient cathedral, and picturesque High Street, fascinated the young Dickens and was indeed 'the birthplace of his fancy' (Forster, 8). He loved dreamily watching the River Medway with 'the great ships standing out to sea or coming home richly laden' and all the other varied shipping described in the 1863 essay 'Chatham Dockyard' (*The Uncommercial Traveller*). Also, it was the little Rochester playhouse that gave him his earliest thrilling experiences of what became one of the master passions of his life, the theatre, as recalled, along with other aspects of the city, in another *Uncommercial Traveller* essay, 'Dullborough Town':

Richard the Third, in a very uncomfortable cloak, had first appeared to me there, and had made my heart leap with terror by backing up against the stage-box in which I was posted, while struggling for life against the virtuous Richmond.

He constantly read and reread the books in his father's little library—the eighteenth-century essayists, *Robinson Crusoe*, *The Vicar of Wakefield*, *Don Quixote*, the works of Fielding and Smollett, and other novels and stories (most notably *The Arabian Nights* and *The Tales of the Genii*). These books made up that 'glorious host' that, as he wrote in the character of the young David when incorporating this real life material into chapter 4 of *David Copperfield*, 'kept alive my fancy' when life turned suddenly very bleak. Indeed, these books became fundamental to his imaginative world, as is clearly attested by the innumerable quotations from, and allusions to, them in all his writings.

In 1822 John Dickens was recalled to London and the family squeezed itself into a smaller house at 16 Bayham Street in the very lower-middle-class suburb of Camden Town. This was a great shock to the young Dickens, who now began hearing much about his father's increasing financial problems. The abrupt termination of his schooling distressed him greatly. Money was found to send Fanny to the Royal Academy of Music but Dickens was left, as he once told his friend and biographer John Forster, to brood bitterly on 'all [he] had lost in losing Chatham' and to yearn 'to [be] taught something anywhere!' (Forster, 9). But he began also to be fascinated by the great world of London, transferring to it 'all the dreaminess and all the romance with which he had invested Chatham' and deriving intense pleasure from being taken for walks in the city, especially anywhere near the slum area of Seven Dials which invariably inspired him with 'wild visions of prodigies of wickedness, want and beggary!' (ibid., 11). Forster characterizes the boy's response to Seven Dials as 'a profound attraction of repulsion' (ibid.), a phrase that goes very much to the heart of the later Dickens's attitude towards grim, squalid, or horrific subjects. John's financial situation continuing to deteriorate, and a rather desperate attempt of Elizabeth's to establish a school for young ladies having failed utterly, he was committed to the Marshalsea debtors' prison on 20 February 1824 and was soon joined there by Elizabeth and the younger children.

Employment had been found for Charles by a family friend at Robert Warren's blacking factory at Hungerford Stairs just off the Strand. There he pasted labels on blacking bottles for 6*s*. a week, lodging first in Little College Street with a Mrs Roylance (on whom he modelled Mrs Pipchin in *Dombey and Son*) and later in Lant Street, Borough, closer to the prison. The deep personal and social outrage, and sense of parental betrayal, that Dickens experienced at the time was a profound grief that he never entirely outgrew, and an intense pity (also intense admiration) for his younger self was to be a mainspring of his fiction from *Oliver Twist* to *Little Dorrit*. In the fragmentary autobiography he wrote in the 1840s, and which Forster incorporated into his biography, he wrote:

> No words can express the secret agony of my soul as I sunk into this companionship [of 'common men and boys']...and felt my early hopes of growing up to be a learned and distinguished man, crushed in my breast. The deep remembrance of the sense I had of being

utterly neglected and hopeless; of the shame I felt in my position; of the misery it was to my young heart to believe that, day by day, what I had learned, and thought, and delighted in, and raised my fancy and my emulation up by, was passing away from me, never to be brought back any more; cannot be written. (Forster, 26)

John Dickens left the prison on 28 May, having been through the insolvency court, and having also received a legacy from his mother, but his son seems to have remained working at the blacking factory for another nine or ten months (Allen, 103). He was finally taken away when John for some reason quarrelled with the proprietor. Elizabeth tried to arrange for the boy's return, for which Dickens never forgave her. John, however, had retired from the pay office on health grounds and was now receiving an Admiralty pension, and said that his son should go back to school. Dickens then became a day boy at the grandly named Wellington House Classical and Commercial Academy in the Hampstead Road, later depicting it and William Jones, its brutal and ignorant proprietor, in *David Copperfield*

('Salem House') and 'Our School' (*Reprinted Pieces*, 1858).

From the day that he entered Jones's school until the day he died he told no one, his wife and his friend Forster alone excepted, about his time in the blacking factory, or about his father's imprisonment. His parents seem likewise to have maintained a total silence on the subject. The first that anyone, the general public or even his own children, knew about these things was when Forster published passages from his unfinished autobiography in the first volume of his *Life of Charles Dickens* (1876). In March 1827 the Dickens family's finances were again in crisis and Dickens's schooling once more ended suddenly. At fifteen he began work as a solicitor's clerk, a humdrum occupation that he found unappealing, though his experiences at both the firms for which he worked (Charles Molloy of Symond's Inn, and Ellis and Blackmore of Raymond Buildings) provided good material for many passages of legal satire in his later sketches and fiction. During his leisure hours he greatly extended and deepened his knowledge of London, London street life, and London popular entertainments. A fellow clerk, George Lear, later recalled, 'I thought I knew

something of the town but after a little talk with
Dickens I found I knew nothing. He knew it all
from Bow to Brentford' (Kitton, 131).

## The young journalist, 1828–1836

By 1828 John Dickens, launched on a new
career as a journalist, had established himself
as a reporter on his brother-in-law's new paper
the *Mirror of Parliament*. Dickens evidently also
decided to try for a career in journalism as
being—potentially, at least—a good deal more
rewarding than drudging on at Ellis and Blackmore's on 15*s*. a week (exactly Bob Cratchit's
wages in *A Christmas Carol*). By fierce appli-
cation, entertainingly recalled in *David Copperfield*, he taught himself Gurney's system of shorthand, and in November 1828 left the lawyers'
office to share a box for freelance reporters in
Doctors' Commons rented by Thomas Charlton, a
distant family connection. It was probably some
time during 1829 that he first met a diminutive
beauty called Maria Beadnell (1810–1886) and
fell headlong in love with her. This passion was
to dominate his emotional life for the next four
years, causing him much torment, not so much
because of the objections that Maria's prosperous

banker father no doubt had about entertaining a struggling young freelance reporter as a prospective son-in-law, but because Maria herself seems to have been of a flirtatious disposition, so that Dickens could never be sure of her real feelings towards him. His steely ambition to make a mark in the world in one way or another was given a keener edge by his passionate desire to make her his wife. He sought to improve himself by reading in the British Museum (Shakespeare and the classics, English and Roman history), having applied for a reader's ticket at the first possible moment, just after his eighteenth birthday. Aware that he had a definite histrionic talent, he also considered the idea of a stage career and obtained (spring 1832) an audition at Covent Garden, but in the event a bad cold prevented him from attending and shortly afterwards came an opportunity to develop his journalistic career.

During 1830 or 1831 Dickens had begun to get work, perhaps as a supernumerary, on his uncle's paper and then in 1832 he was taken on to the regular staff of a new evening paper, the *True Sun*. He rapidly acquired a reputation as an outstanding parliamentary reporter and, having inherited to the full his father's love of convivial occasions, pursued at the same time an energetic social life. In April 1833, anticipating a favourite activity of his later years, he organized some elaborate private theatricals at his parents' home in Bentinck Street. Shortly afterwards came the final cruel collapse of all hopes of winning Maria's heart. The intense pain this caused him left a permanent scar on his emotional life, although he was able to present Maria and his ardent youthful love for her in a comic-sentimental light in the Dora episodes of *David Copperfield*. Many years later he wrote to her that 'the wasted tenderness of those hard years' had bred in him 'a habit of suppression ... which I know is no part of my original nature, but which makes me chary of showing my affections, even to my children, except when they are very young' (*Letters*, 7.543).

In December 1833 Dickens's first published literary work appeared in the *Monthly Magazine*; it was a farcical little story of middle-class manners called 'A Dinner at Poplar Walk' (later retitled as 'Mr Minns and his Cousin'). Over the next year it was followed, in the same periodical (the owner of which, a Captain Holland, could not offer any payment) by several other stories in a similar vein, for the sixth of which Dickens first used the pen-name Boz (derived from his little brother Augustus's mispronunciation of Moses, his Goldsmithian family nickname). Dickens's appointment, in August 1834, to the reporting staff of the leading whig newspaper, the *Morning Chronicle*, at a salary of 5 guineas per week, placed his career on a firm footing and he was soon distinguishing himself not only as a brilliant shorthand writer but also as a most effective and efficient special correspondent, reporting provincial elections and other events, and being exhilarated by the keen competition provided by the *Times* correspondent. In September he began to contribute a series of 'Street Sketches', illustrative of everyday London life, to the *Chronicle*. These attracted favourable notice and his offer to write, for extra pay, a similar series, twenty 'Sketches of London', for the newly founded sister paper the *Evening Chronicle*, was welcomed by that paper's editor, George Hogarth. The first, 'Hackney Coach Stands', appeared in January 1835 and the last, 'Our Parish (the Ladies' Societies)', in August 1835. Dickens then began yet another series, twelve 'Scenes and Characters', in *Bell's Life in London*. The last of these, 'The Streets at Night', appeared in January 1836, to be swiftly followed by a collected two-volume edition, *Sketches by*

*Boz*, published by John Macrone and illustrated by the renowned comic artist George Cruik-shank. Dickens probably owed his introduction to Macrone and Cruikshank to William Harrison Ainsworth who had become a close friend, pro-viding Dickens with his first entrée into literary circles.

The two-volume edition of *Sketches by Boz*, for which Dickens specially wrote two non-comic pieces, 'A Visit to Newgate' and 'The Black Veil', was extremely well received. The sketches were praised for their humour, wit, touches of pathos, and the 'startling fidelity' of their descriptions of London life (Collins, *Critical Heritage*, 30). Mean-while, he continued with all his routine journal-istic work and coped as best he could with his father's recurring financial crises, helped by close friends like his fellow journalist Thomas Beard, who was to remain a lifelong and much loved friend, and the young lawyer Thomas Mitton, who acted as his solicitor for many years. He took lodg-ings for himself and his fourteen-year-old brother Fred in Furnival's Inn, Holborn. By this time he had become acquainted with George Hogarth's family and had become attracted to the eldest daughter, Catherine (1816–1879), though without the passionate intensity that had characterized his love for Maria Beadnell, and he became engaged to her during the summer of 1835. Catherine was small and pretty like Maria, with blue eyes and brown hair—also gentle, amiable, and proficient in many of the so-called 'accomplishments' expected of young ladies at this time.

# Fame

**2**

## Pickwick and marriage

In February 1836, just after the appearance of the two-volume *Sketches by Boz*, two young booksellers who were moving into publishing, Edward Chapman and William Hall, approached Dickens to write the letterpress for a series of steel-engraved plates by the popular comic artist Robert Seymour. The plates, depicting the misadventures of a group of cockney sportsmen, were to be published in twenty monthly numbers, each containing four plates. They offered Dickens £14 a month for the work, an 'emolument' that was, as he wrote to Catherine, 'too tempting to resist' (*Letters*, 1.129). He accepted the commission despite Ainsworth's warning that he would demean himself by participating in such a 'low' form of publication, but stipulated that he should be allowed to widen the scope of the proposed subject 'with a freer range of English scenes and people'. He then, he later recalled, 'thought of Mr Pickwick, and wrote the first number' ('Preface' to the Cheap Edition of *Pickwick*, 1847). This appeared on 31 March 1836 and on 2 April Dickens and Catherine were married at St Luke's, Chelsea. They spent their honeymoon in the Kentish village of Chalk and then set up home in the new and more spacious chambers Dickens had taken in Furnival's Inn where he was already established. On 20 April Seymour committed suicide but the publishers boldly decided to continue the series, despite disappointing initial sales.

Seymour was replaced, after the brief trial of R. W. Buss, with a young artist, Hablot Knight Browne (Phiz), who was Dickens's main illustrator for the next twenty-three years. In recognition of the fact that Dickens was now very much the senior partner in the enterprise, the number of plates was halved, the letterpress increased from twenty-eight to thirty-two pages, and his monthly remuneration rose to £21. With the introduction of Sam Weller in the fourth number sales began to increase dramatically and soon

*Pickwick* was the greatest publishing sensation since Byron had woken to find himself famous, as a result of the publication of the first two cantos of *Childe Harold*, in 1812. By the end of its run in November 1837 Dickens's monthly serial had a phenomenal circulation of nearly 40,000 and had earned the publishers £14,000, an appreciable amount of which would have stemmed from the fees paid by advertisers who supplied inserts or took space in the 'Pickwick Advertiser' that eventually occupied twenty-four extra pages each month. The depiction of the benevolent old innocent Mr Pickwick and the streetwise but good-hearted Sam Weller as a sort of latter-day Don Quixote and Sancho Panza, the rich evocation of that pre-railway, pre-Reform Bill England that was so rapidly disappearing, the idyll of Dingley Dell, the sparkling social comedy and hilarious legal satire, the comic and pathetic scenes in the Fleet prison, the astonishing variety of vividly evoked and utterly distinct characters, the bravura wit and, above all, that 'endless fertility in laughter-causing detail' that Walter Bagehot later called 'Mr Dickens's most astonishing peculiarity' (Collins, *Critical Heritage*, 395)—all these things combined to give *The Pickwick Papers* a phenomenal popularity that transcended barriers of class, age, and education. The playwright Mary Russell Mitford wrote to an Irish friend, 'All the boys and girls talk [Dickens's] fun—the boys in the street; and yet those who are of the higher taste like it the most.... Lord Denman studies *Pickwick* on the bench while the jury are deliberating' (ibid., 36).

Dickens could hardly have anticipated success on this scale or he would probably not have committed himself to so many other projects such as turning one of his sketches into a two-act 'burletta', *The Strange Gentleman*, as a vehicle for the comedian John Pritt Harley. It was successfully produced at the St James's Theatre (9 September 1836) and ran for fifty nights. He also wrote, under the pseudonym Timothy Sparks, an anti-sabbatarian pamphlet, *Sunday under Three Heads*, the precursor of many later attacks on what he saw as blatantly hypocritical and class-biased legislative proposals. By late October he had clearly decided that he would be able to live by his pen and resigned from his *Morning Chronicle* post.

Dickens was, in fact, grotesquely over-committed to publishers who were all eager to sign up the

dazzling new literary star. He accepted Richard
Bentley's invitation to edit a new monthly magazine, *Bentley's Miscellany*, to begin publication
in the new year, being already committed to
write two three-volume novels for Bentley, as
well as a third novel, *Gabriel Vardon, the Lock-
smith of London*, for Macrone, and another (as yet
unnamed) work of the same length and nature
as *Pickwick* for Chapman and Hall. He had been
at work, with J. P. Hullah, on a rather vapid
operetta, *The Village Coquettes*, which was produced at the St James's on 6 December but had
only a short run, and throughout 1836 he had
been publishing more sketches in the *Morning
Chronicle* and elsewhere, including some of his
finest work in this genre, such as 'Meditations
in Monmouth Street'. These sketches, together
with earlier ones still uncollected, were gathered
up in the one-volume *Sketches by Boz: Second
Series* published by Macrone on 17 December.
This volume ended with an item written specially for it, a Grand Guignol piece called 'The
Drunkard's Death'. About this time Dickens first
met (probably through Ainsworth) John Forster,
a young theatre critic, literary reviewer, and historian, who had moved to London from New-
castle and was already very much in the swim of

the metropolitan literary world. Forster became one of Dickens's most intimate friends and his lifelong trusted literary adviser—even to some extent collaborator, since from October 1837 he read everything that Dickens wrote, either in manuscript or proof—as well as his chosen biographer. Forster's legal training and expertise made him an invaluable ally in Dickens's many disputes with publishers, the first of which was with Macrone to whom Dickens had sold the copyright of *Sketches by Boz* as part of a deal to release himself from the promise to write *Gabriel Vardon*. Macrone sought to profit from the success of *Pickwick* by proposing to issue both series of the *Sketches* in twenty monthly parts. Dickens strongly objected and tried through Forster's agency to dissuade Macrone. In the end, Chapman and Hall bought the copyright from Macrone for a substantial sum and themselves issued *Sketches* in monthly parts from November 1837 to June 1839, with additional Cruikshank plates and with pink covers to distinguish the work from *Pickwick* in its green monthly covers. At the conclusion of this serialization, the *Sketches* were published in one volume, described on the title-page as a 'new edition, complete'.

The first number of *Bentley's Miscellany*, edited by 'Boz' and with illustrations by Cruikshank, came out in January 1837 and in February appeared the first instalment of Dickens's new story, *Oliver Twist, or, The Parish Boy's Progress*, which ran in the journal for twenty-four months (during the first ten of which Dickens was also still writing a monthly *Pickwick*). *Oliver Twist* was originally conceived as a satire on the new poor law of 1834 which herded the destitute and the helpless into harshly run union workhouses, and which was perceived by Dickens as a monstrously unjust and inhumane piece of legislation (he was still fiercely attacking it in *Our Mutual Friend* in 1865). Once the scene shifted to London, however, *Oliver Twist* developed into a unique and compelling blend of a 'realistic' tale about thieves and prostitutes and a melodrama with strong metaphysical overtones. The pathos of little Oliver (the first of many such child figures in Dickens), the farcical comedy of the Bumbles, the sinister fascination of Fagin, the horror of Nancy's murder, and the powerful evocation of London's dark and labyrinthine criminal underworld, all helped to drive Dickens's popularity to new heights.

But there was mounting tension between himself and Bentley because of the latter's constant interference with Dickens's editorial freedom and his quibbles over the extent of Dickens's own contributions. Bentley also irritated Dickens by pressing for the delivery of a new novel (that is, the *Gabriel Vardon* originally contracted to Macrone, now renamed *Barnaby Rudge*; Dickens, having bought himself out of the arrangement with Macrone, had now signed a contract for the book with Bentley). Sometimes the relationship temporarily improved, as in November 1837, when Dickens agreed to edit for Bentley the memoirs of the great clown Joey Grimaldi (published with an 'Introductory chapter' and a concluding one by Dickens, and wonderful illustrations by Cruikshank, in February 1838), but at last came a complete rupture and Dickens resigned the editorship of the *Miscellany* in the January 1839 number. By the summer of 1840 he was fully committed to Chapman and Hall as his sole publishers, having gradually disentangled himself— with their help, and that of Forster—from all commitments to Macrone and Bentley, the latter now usually referred to by Dickens in very uncomplimentary terms ('the Vagabond', 'the Burlington Street Brigand', and so on).

The promised *Pickwick*-style work for Chapman and Hall, now carrying the very eighteenth-century-style title of *The Life and Adventures of Nicholas Nickleby*, had begun its monthly part-issue in March 1838 and was completed in twenty numbers in October 1839. This story, which for thirteen months Dickens wrote alongside *Oliver Twist*, originated in his determination to expose the scandal of unwanted children consigned to remote and brutal Yorkshire schools; accompanied by Browne, he conducted an on-the-spot mid-winter investigation just before beginning to write *Nickleby*. In this rambling, episodic, often wildly funny book, written very much in the mode of the Smollett novels Dickens had devoured as a child, the Yorkshire school setting is soon left behind, and the gallant young hero and his pathetic protégé, Smike, wander forth to undergo various adventures, both farcical and melodramatic; they are persecuted by Nicholas's wicked uncle and other villains, who also threaten the virtue of Nicholas's pure young sister Kate, but all is eventually set right by the benevolent Cheeryble brothers, though they cannot save Smike. The story is rich in unforgettable comic characters like the endlessly garrulous Mrs Nickleby and the strolling player Vincent Crummles and his troupe, and in places it resembles *Sketches by Boz* in its vivid evocation of particular London neighbourhoods.

Just before Dickens began *Oliver Twist*, he and Catherine had had their first child, Charles Culliford Boz Dickens (1837–1896), in January 1837, and had shortly afterwards moved from their Furnival's Inn chambers to a new house, 48 Doughty Street (now the Charles Dickens Museum); Dickens bought a three-year lease and paid £80 a year in rent. Staying with them was Catherine's younger sister Mary Hogarth, whose sudden death on 7 May, aged only seventeen ('Young, beautiful and Good' according to the epitaph Dickens composed for her headstone in Kensal Green cemetery), was a devastating blow to Dickens—so great, indeed, that he had to suspend the writing of both *Pickwick* and *Oliver Twist* for a month, a unique occurrence in his career. He had lost, he wrote, 'the dearest friend I ever had', one who sympathized 'with all my thoughts and feelings more than any one I knew ever did or will', declaring also, 'I solemnly believe that so perfect a creature never breathed' (*Letters*, 1.263, 629, 259). It was the third great emotional crisis of his life, following the blacking factory experience and the Beadnell affair, and one that profoundly influenced him as an artist as well as a man.

In all other respects Dickens's life, both professional and personal, during the later 1830s became steadily more prosperous. The sales of *Nickleby* 'were satisfactory—highly so' (Patten, 98) and Chapman and Hall were happy to fall in with his plans for editing a weekly miscellany to be called *Master Humphrey's Clock*, for which he would receive a weekly salary of £50 as well as a half-share of net profits. He formed close and lasting friendships with many leading figures in the world of the arts, notably the 'eminent tragedian' William Charles Macready (always a particularly loved and honoured friend), the painters Daniel Maclise and Clarkson Stanfield, the lawyer and dramatist Thomas Noon Talfourd, and the poet Walter Savage Landor; he was elected to both the Garrick and the Athenaeum clubs, invited to Lady Blessington's salon, and lionized generally. He also became acquainted with Thomas Carlyle, whom he greatly revered, and who profoundly influenced his thinking on social matters. He once said, 'I would go at all times farther to see Carlyle than any man alive' (Forster, 839). Carlyle's first impression of Dickens was that he was 'a quiet, shrewd-looking, little fellow, who seems to guess pretty well what he is and what others are' (*Letters*, 2.141). Maclise painted the twenty-eight-year-old Dickens's portrait as an elegant young writer and the portrait was engraved as the frontispiece to the volume edition of *Nickleby*. At the end of 1839 the growing Dickens family (Mary, always known as Mamie, was born in 1838, Kate Macready in 1839) moved into a much grander house, 1 Devonshire Terrace, Marylebone, near to Regent's Park. Dickens paid £800 for an eleven-year lease and an annual rent of £160. From 1837 onwards the family spent several weeks each summer at the little Kentish resort of Broadstairs, later described in *Household Words* as 'Our Watering Place' ('Our English Watering Place' in *Reprinted Pieces*, 1858). Here Dickens would entertain friends but would also continue working, dashing up to London from time to time for business or social occasions.

### *The Old Curiosity Shop* and *Barnaby Rudge*, 1840–1841

*Master Humphrey's Clock* began publication on 4 April 1840. Initial sales were very large but quickly declined when the public realized the *Clock* was not to be a continuous story. The reclusive old cripple Master Humphrey and his little club of old-fashioned story-tellers did not appeal to the public and even the reintroduction of Mr Pickwick and the Wellers failed to halt the sharp decline in sales. The woodcut illustrations by Cattermole and Browne dropped into the text that were such a feature of the *Clock* made it an expensive product, so some prompt action was needed. Dickens quickly developed one of an intended series of 'Personal Adventures of Master Humphrey' into a full-length story and this, under the title *The Old Curiosity Shop*, soon took over the entire publication. The story of Little Nell's wanderings about England with her helpless old grandfather, fleeing from Quilp, a grotesquely hideous, anarchic, and sexually predatory dwarf, is the most Romantic and fairy tale-like of Dickens's novels, and it also contains, in the story of Dick Swiveller and the Brasses' little slavey, the Marchioness, some of the greatest humorous passages that Dickens ever wrote. By the end of the story's serialization in the *Clock* (6 February 1841) the circulation had reached a phenomenal 100,000 copies. Nell's slow decline and eventual (off-stage) beatified death plunged this vast readership into grief and mourning, Lord Jeffrey famously declaring that there had been 'nothing so good as Nell since Cordelia' (Forster, 174). For Dickens himself it reopened an old wound: 'Dear Mary died yesterday, when I think of this sad story' (*Letters*, 2.182). The *Shop* was immediately succeeded in the *Clock* by the long projected *Barnaby Rudge*, Dickens's first historical novel, dealing with the anti-Catholic Gordon riots of 1780 and written in conscious emulation of Sir Walter Scott. The Wordsworthian influence, evident in some parts of *The Old Curiosity Shop*, is also seen here in the conception of Barnaby which clearly owes something to Wordsworth's Idiot Boy as well as to Davie Gellatley in Scott's *Waverley*.

The completion of *Barnaby* (27 November 1841) 'worked off the last of the commitments so hastily entered into in the heady days of 1836' (Patten, 118), ending five years of intensive labour which saw Dickens established as far and away the most popular writer in Britain, though he was somewhat bitterly aware that he was still making much more money for his publishers than for himself. The triumphal welcome he received in Edinburgh in June 1841, following an invitation to go there from Lord Jeffrey and other distinguished Scottish admirers, was a striking manifestation of the extraordinary public position this young writer now occupied. The dinner in his honour was, he told Forster, 'the most brilliant affair you can conceive' (Forster, 176). He himself spoke, in the two toasts he proposed, with notable effect and eloquence, as he was so often to do in later life as the star turn at other banquets, meetings, charitable dinners, and so on. Four days later he was given the freedom of the city, after which he and Catherine went on a scenic tour that took them as far north as Glencoe; they returned into England via Abbotsford in order to visit Scott's house. The history of Scott's being forced by financial circumstances in his later years to maintain a prolific output was in Dickens's mind when he now proposed to Chapman and Hall that, after the cessation of the *Clock* on 27 November (*Barnaby Rudge* had not gripped the reading public in the way that *The Old Curiosity Shop* had, and the magazine's circulation had fallen to 30,000), he should have a sabbatical year. By continuing to write incessantly he would, he feared, do 'what every other successful man has done' and make himself 'too cheap' (*Letters*, 2.365).

Wisely submitting to their hugely lucrative author's wishes, Chapman and Hall agreed to pay Dickens £150 a month for fourteen months as an advance on his profits from his next work (to be published in monthly numbers). He was soon being 'haunted by visions of America, night and day' (Forster, 195) and, Catherine's deep reluctance to leave the children having been overborne, resolved that they should make a six-months' tour there, the children to be left under Macready's care. He would keep a notebook on his travels, and Chapman and Hall should publish it on his return. His eager preparations for the trip, excited as he was by communications like Washington Irving's telling him 'it would be such a triumph from one of the States to the other, as was never known in any Nation' (*Letters*, 2.383), were briefly interrupted by a painful operation for a fistula. He soon recovered, polished off the last numbers of the *Clock* (the final number appeared on 4 December), and engaged in a whirl of pre-embarkation social engagements.

## America and its aftermath, 1842

On 4 January Dickens and Catherine embarked on the steamship *Britannia* which, after a terrifying crossing, reached Halifax, Nova Scotia, on 19 January. Next day Dickens was both fêted by the local dignitaries and cheered by crowds in the streets. He and Catherine then re-embarked and landed (on 22 January) at Boston, where they put up at the Tremont House Hotel. Exhilarated by his initial experience of America, Dickens soon began to find, however, that the surging crowds of admirers who intruded themselves on him and Catherine at all hours were both exhausting and frustrating, and the tremendous flood of correspondence that came pouring in on him was simply overwhelming. To help him cope with the situation he hired a young art student, George Washington Putnam, nicknamed 'Q', as his secretary and travelling companion. He had met Putnam when sitting for his portrait to Francis Alexander (he sat also, but this time for a bust, to another local artist, Henry Dexter).

In Boston, Dickens carried out the first of those investigative visits to prisons, asylums, and other public institutions that became such a feature of his American journey, and he met many notables, among them the celebrated poet Henry Wadsworth Longfellow and Cornelius Felton, professor of Greek at Harvard, both of whom became much-loved friends. At a public banquet in his honour (on 1 February) he spoke with passion of having 'dreamed by day and night, for years, of setting foot upon this shore, and breathing this pure air' (*Speeches*, ed. Fielding, 19) but also touched briefly on the vexed question of the absence of any international copyright agreement between Britain and America, allowing the wholesale pirating of his own and other British authors' work by American newspapers. He and Catherine went on to New York via Worcester, Massachusetts, Hartford, Connecticut, and New Haven. Speaking at another banquet in his honour in Hartford (on 8 February), he again referred to the international copyright question. In New York he and Catherine stayed at the Carlton House Hotel (from 12 February to 5 March). The whirlwind of celebrity continued to engulf them, its most spectacular manifestation being the great 'Boz ball' at the Park Theatre (on 14 February) which Dickens called 'a most superb affair' (Forster, 215).

Shortly afterwards, however, lying ill in his hotel room, he wrote to Jonathan Chapman, mayor of Boston, 'I am sick to death of the life I have been leading here—worn out in mind and body', and inveighed against the newspapers for attacking him over international copyright 'in such terms of vagabond scurrility as they would denounce no murderer with' (*Letters*, 2.76–7). Press attacks on his 'mercenariness' and bad taste in speaking about money matters at gatherings in his honour were indeed often couched in crudely offensive terms. Dickens's romantic dream of America as a pure, free, 'innocent' land, untrammelled by the corrupt institutions and the pernicious snobberies and class hatreds of the Old World, was rapidly turning sour, and he resolved to decline all future invitations of a public nature. He and Catherine went on to Philadelphia, where he encountered Edgar Allan Poe, and where, despite his resolve, he found himself duped into holding a 'levee' at his hotel for 600 people. From there they went to Washington where Dickens saw congress in session and had a very low-key meeting with President John Tyler. During an excursion south to Richmond, Virginia, his increasing disillusion-ment with America was intensified by the shock and disgust he experienced at seeing slavery at first hand. From Baltimore he wrote to Macready, 'This is not the Republic I came to see. This is not the Republic of my imagination. I infinitely prefer a liberal Monarchy—even with its sickening accompaniments of Court Circulars...to such a Government as this' (*Letters*, 3.156).

The travellers proceeded by rail, stagecoach, and (disconcertingly unhygienic) canal boat to Pittsburgh, then by steamboat down the Ohio to Cincinnati, thence to Louisville and Cairo (the horrible 'Eden' of *Martin Chuzzlewit*), and then up the Mississippi (which Dickens thought 'the beastliest river in the world', Forster, 259) to St Louis. After returning to Cincinnati, Dickens and Catherine headed north via Columbus, Ohio, to Buffalo and Niagara Falls, where they stayed from 26 April to 4 May. The falls impressed Dickens profoundly. He wrote of them, 'It would be hard for a man to stand nearer to God than he does here' and expressed a belief that the spirit of Mary Hogarth had 'been there many times, I doubt not, since her sweet face faded from my earthly sight' (Forster, 270). There followed a four-week tour in Canada, where Dickens felt considerably more at home than in America. He visited Toronto, Kingston, Montreal, and Quebec, and in Montreal took great delight in organizing, and participating in, some elaborate amateur theatricals involving the officers of the local garrison. Catherine also took a part and, Dickens wrote to Forster, acted 'devilish well, I assure you!' (ibid., 276). By now, however, both Dickens and Catherine were desperately homesick. She had proved herself, Dickens told Forster, 'a *most admirable* traveller in every respect . . . has always accommodated herself, well and cheerfully, to everything . . . and proved herself perfectly game' (ibid., 266), but she could now no longer contain her eagerness to see the children again. The travellers returned to New York and, after a final expedition to see a Shaker village in Lebanon and to West Point, happily embarked on 7 June on a sailing packet (they had had enough of steamships), the *George Washington*. They landed at Liverpool on 29 June and went straight on to London for an ecstatic reunion with the children. Hardly less joyous were Dickens's reunions with his friends Forster, Macready, Maclise, Stanfield, and others but he soon had to buckle down to the writing of his promised American travel book. The furore over international copyright continued, fed by a circular letter Dickens wrote on the topic (on 7 July) which got into American newspapers alongside a forged letter in which he was maliciously represented as branding America a country of gross manners and squalid money-making. There was copious and vehement editorializing about this seemingly clear evidence of Dickens's snobbishness and ingratitude.

Against this background he wrote his promised travel book for Chapman and Hall, *American Notes, for General Circulation* (2 vols.), which appeared on 19 October. In it Dickens praised many of America's public institutions but condemned the national worship of 'smartness' (that is, sharp practice), and attacked particularly the hypocrisy and venality of the American press. He also commented unfavourably on many aspects of American social life, notably the widespread habit of spitting in public, and, predictably, denounced slavery at some length. *American Notes* sold well but attracted little favourable comment in Britain (Macaulay deemed it 'at once frivolous and dull'; Collins, *Critical Heritage*, 124) and, unsurprisingly, it met with a very hostile reception in the American press. Meanwhile, Dickens, having enjoyed the usual summer sojourn with his family in Broadstairs (now included as a permanent member of the family was his fifteen-year-old sister-in-law Georgina Hogarth), began turning his mind to the twenty-monthly-number novel he was contracted to write for Chapman and Hall.

Having an idea, in the event not followed up, that he might open the story on the coast of Cornwall, he made what was evidently an exceedingly jolly expedition to that county together with Forster, Maclise, and Stanfield (from 27 October to 4 November).

# Society, charity, and satire 3

## Critic of society

*Martin Chuzzlewit* was published in monthly parts from 31 December 1842 to 30 June 1844. Dickens thought it 'in a hundred points immeasurably the best of my stories' (Forster, 305), and declared that he felt his power more than ever before. And, indeed, this is the great transitional novel that leads from the dazzling farce and comedy of humours, the often powerfully effective melodrama and satirical episodes, the sometimes startling grotesquerie and the picaresque pleasures of the early fiction to the complex, resonant, carefully planned and structured masterpieces of Dickens's later years. He had for the first time a conscious overall design, 'to show, more or less by every person introduced, the number and variety of humours and vices that have their root in selfishness' (ibid., 291), and the superb 'humour' characters of Pecksniff and Mrs Gamp as well as the squalid murderer Jonas Chuzzlewit are all very much a part of this design, though they also transcend it. The early 1840s were a bad time for publishing, however, and sales were disappointing. Even Dickens's decision to send his hero to America in the sixth monthly number and his lively satirizing of American manners and institutions failed to push the circulation much above 20,000. Meanwhile, as a man with a highly active social conscience, and mindful always of that desperate time in his own childhood when he 'lounged about the streets, insufficiently and unsatisfactorily fed' and might so easily, he felt, have become 'for any care that was taken of me, a little robber or a little vagabond' (ibid., 28), Dickens was becoming ever more urgently concerned about the plight of the children of the poor. He was horrified by revelations in a parliamentary commissioners' report about the condition of children employed in mines and factories, and interested himself strongly in the Ragged School movement, particularly in persuading the millionaire philanthropist Angela Burdett-Coutts (with whom he had been friendly since 1839) to give financial support to the Field Lane School in the area of London where he had earlier located Fagin's lair in *Oliver Twist*. Disgusted by the squabbles between Anglicans, Catholics, and nonconformists that bedevilled the debate about public education, he joined the Unitarians, remaining a member for three or four years before returning to Anglicanism.

In October 1843 Dickens had the sudden inspiration of writing a Christmas story intended to open its readers' hearts towards those struggling to survive on the lower rungs of the economic ladder and to encourage practical benevolence, but also to warn of the terrible danger to society created by the toleration of widespread ignorance and actual want among the poor. The result, written at white heat, was *A Christmas Carol: in Prose*, published by Chapman and Hall on 19 December as a handsomely bound little volume with four hand-coloured illustrations by John Leech, price 5*s*. This 'Ghost Story of Christmas', as it was subtitled, was a sensational success. The story of the archetypal miser Scrooge's conversion to benevolence by supernatural means, and the resulting preservation of the poor crippled child, Tiny Tim ('who did NOT die'), was greeted with almost universal delight (in the February 1844 number of *Fraser's* Thackeray called it 'a national benefit and to every man or woman who reads it a personal kindness'). But it had been expensive to produce and Dickens's profits from it were very moderate.

This so exacerbated the sorry state of his relations with Chapman and Hall (already strained by an unfortunate comment of William Hall's arising from the poor sales of the initial monthly numbers of *Chuzzlewit*) that he determined to break with them completely. He invited his printers, Bradbury and Evans, to become his new publishers and they—somewhat reluctantly on account of their inexperience as publishers—agreed. Dickens was further vexed by the highly unsatisfactory outcome of his prosecution of a cheap publishing concern for blatant piracy of the *Carol* (he had long suffered from gross and widespread exploitation of his work by hack dramatists and gutter publishers). He won his case, but the pirates simply went bankrupt and he was left to pay his own costs. By May 1844 he had agreed with Bradbury and Evans terms by which they were to advance him a total of £3800 in return for a quarter-share in whatever he might write over the next eight years, including a successor to the *Carol* for Christmas 1844.

*45*

SOCIETY, CHARITY, AND SATIRE

## European travels, 1844–1847

In July 1844 Dickens moved his entire household (a fifth child, Francis Jeffrey, had been born in January) to Genoa, having decided to live abroad for a year, partly as an economy (it was cheaper to live in the splendid Palazzo Peschiere in Genoa than in Devonshire Terrace), partly to escape the increasing demands on his time at home, and partly for the stimulus of new scenes. He made a midwinter dash back to London, via Venice and Milan, to read the *Carol*'s more overtly political successor, *The Chimes*, to Forster and a group of other friends, including Carlyle and Douglas Jerrold. During 1845 Dickens and Catherine travelled to Rome, Naples, and Florence, Georgina joining them in Naples (where they made a hazardous ascent of Vesuvius). In Genoa and elsewhere he became intensely involved in using, either directly or long-distance, the power of mesmeric healing he discovered in himself to alleviate the condition of Mme de la Rue, an Englishwoman who suffered great distress from hallucinations. This strange intimacy with Mme de la Rue caused Catherine considerable uneasiness, not surprisingly. Dickens's response was righteous indignation (eight years later, when he again met the de la Rues abroad, he wrote home to Catherine admonishing her that he thought it would become her now to write Mme de la Rue a friendly letter, which she obediently did). The Dickens family were back in London in July 1845 and Dickens energetically set about organizing a production of Ben Jonson's *Every Man in his Humour* to be given by a band of his literary and artistic friends, the Amateur Players. This took place on 21 September in a private theatre in Dean Street, Dickens's own virtuoso performance as Captain Bobadil winning many plaudits. He had an understanding with Bradbury and Evans that he might start a new weekly magazine jointly with them and he had canvassed Forster with the idea of one to be called *The Cricket* (the title was revived a few months later for his third Christmas book, *The Cricket on the Hearth*). In the event, however, it was Bradbury and Evans's new national newspaper the *Daily News* that he agreed to edit. Liberal in politics and intended specifically to promote the railway interest, the paper first appeared on 21 January 1846. Even Dickens's phenomenal energy proved unequal to editing a national daily on top of all his other commitments, however, and he resigned on 9 February. But he continued to write for the paper, notably a series of 'Travelling Letters' (21 January–11 March), describing his recent journey through France and sojourn in Italy, and five letters (23 February–16 March) powerfully arguing against capital punishment. The 'Travelling Letters' formed the basis of his second travel book, *Pictures from Italy* (published in May 1846 with four illustrations by Samuel Palmer), notable for its anti-Catholic bias, which was no doubt the reason for the withdrawal of the artist originally commissioned to illustrate it, Clarkson Stanfield.

In June Dickens once again moved his whole household abroad (a sixth child, Alfred D'Orsay Tennyson, had been born in October 1845). This time he settled in Lausanne, where he quickly formed a congenial circle of Swiss and English friends, finished writing a version of the New Testament intended solely for his children's use and not for publication (it was eventually published in 1934 under the title *The Life of Our Lord*), and began work on his new novel *Dombey and Son*, published in twenty monthly numbers from

30 September 1846 to 31 March 1848. Though hampered by not being able to walk London's crowded streets (that great 'magic lantern', as he called it, so necessary to his imagination; Forster, 423), and also by having to write his Christmas book for 1846, *The Battle of Life*, he nevertheless made excellent progress with the novel. *Dombey* 'was to do with Pride what its predecessor had done with selfishness' (ibid., 471) but was far more carefully planned and structured than *Chuzzlewit* and is now recognized as one of the greatest of all his works.

It is the first novel for which a full set of working notes and number-plans survives (in the Forster collection, Victoria and Albert Museum). It is also the first one to have an explicitly contemporary setting. The railway features strongly in the story, which is also much concerned with the fate of women in contemporary middle-class English society. From the start the sales of *Dombey* were extremely good, outstripping those of *Chuzzlewit* by 10,000 copies, and it is with this novel that Dickens's financial anxieties ceased and he began to be able to build up a solid prosperity. He moved the family to Paris for the winter of 1846–7, then back to London by March for the launch of the first collected edition of his works, the so-called Cheap Edition (published in weekly, monthly, and volume form), the birth of Sydney Smith Haldiman Dickens (18 April), and more activity by the Amateur Players with the object of raising funds for a pension for the poet and journalist Leigh Hunt. Dickens repeated his Bobadil triumph in performances of *Every Man in his Humour* at Manchester and Liverpool (26, 28 July), and also took energetic leading roles in the various one-act farces played as afterpieces.

## Dickens's 'favourite child'

As the writing of *Dombey* proceeded Dickens was also devoting tremendous energy to the setting up of a home for homeless women, funded by Miss Burdett-Coutts, and intended for the rehabilitation of women who had fallen into prostitution or petty crime. Urania Cottage (named after Venus Urania) opened at Shepherd's Bush in west London in November 1847 and for the next ten years Dickens was very active in all aspects of its administration, in recruiting suitable inmates and arranging for their training in domestic skills, maintaining discipline, and in arranging for the sending of successful 'graduates' of the home to start new lives in Australia (as does the reclaimed prostitute Martha in *David Copperfield*) or South Africa. After finishing *Dombey* Dickens once again threw himself into organizing, on behalf of a variety of good causes, many other performances by the Amateur Players (Shakespeare's *Merry Wives of Windsor* with Dickens as Shallow being now added to the repertory) in London, Birmingham, Manchester, Liverpool, Edinburgh, and Glasgow.

Beneath all the social whirl and charitable activities of Dickens's mid- to late thirties there seems to have lain a growing preoccupation with his earlier years, traces of which may be clearly seen in parts of *Dombey*. He began (probably during 1847–8) writing his autobiography for posthumous publication but, according to his own later account, destroyed it when his narrative reached the episode of his love for Maria Beadnell since that was, he found, still a source of too much pain to him to allow him to describe it. If he did, in fact, burn the whole manuscript as he claimed, he must have begun the projected autobiography again later since Forster quotes extensively from an (apparently incomplete) manuscript near the beginning of his *Life of Dickens*, a manuscript that he (Forster) presumably subsequently destroyed. Dickens's fifth and last Christmas book, *The Haunted Man* (1848), is preoccupied with memory and its relationship to the moral life, especially in the dealing with persisting memories of wrongs and sorrows.

Dickens was evidently beginning to think of his next novel in *Bildungsroman* terms—that is, the story of a young man's life from infancy to maturity—and named his sixth son (*b.* January 1849) after Henry Fielding 'in a kind of homage to the style of work he was now so bent on beginning' (Forster, 524). *David Copperfield* (published 30 April 1849–31 October 1850), follows on naturally from all the foregoing. It is Dickens's first first-person novel (David as narrator calls it 'my written memory') and in it he draws, much more directly than hitherto, on events and people from his own personal life in 'a very complicated interweaving of truth and fiction' (ibid., 497). The misery of the blacking factory days (his notes for writing the number describing little David labouring in Murdstone and Grinby's bottling factory contain the poignant phrase 'What I know so well'), the details of his career as a young journalist, and the raptures of his love for Maria

Beadnell are all presented with only the lightest fictional disguise. In depicting the Micawbers and their recurrent crises Dickens draws on the personalities and former financial problems of his parents. Although the novel's initial sales were rather lower than those of *Dombey*, *Copperfield* received considerable critical acclaim and before long was widely held to be his greatest work. Undoubtedly it became for very many readers, then as now, his best-loved novel, an opinion in which Dickens himself coincided, calling it in a preface to the book of 1867 his 'favourite child'.

## *Household Words*

During 1848–9 Dickens wrote frequently and, like all other contributors, anonymously for the distinguished radical weekly *The Examiner*, edited by Forster since 1847. He had earlier written several reviews for the journal but now supplied, besides further reviews, several fiercely polemical pieces on contemporary social issues such as the growth of ritualism in the Anglican church, the temperance movement's campaign, and the Tooting baby farm scandal (on which he wrote no fewer than four scathing articles). On 30 March 1850 appeared the first number of his own long-meditated weekly journal, *House-hold Words*, which he co-owned with Bradbury and Evans, Wills, and Forster (Dickens owned 50 per cent of the shares, the publishers 25 per cent, Forster 12.5 per cent, and Dickens's sub-editor William Henry Wills another 12.5 per cent). Dickens also received an editorial salary of £500 p.a. and payment for his own contributions. Wills was a highly efficient and resourceful sub-editor and was for the next eighteen years Dickens's trusted right-hand man and confidential man of business.

*Household Words* proclaimed itself at every opening as 'Conducted by Charles Dickens'; all non-fictional contributions, however, including his own, were published anonymously. The journal's weekly twenty-four double-columned, unillustrated pages cost 2*d.* and featured a mix of informative and entertaining articles as well as social and political satire, and serialized fiction. Elizabeth Gaskell and Wilkie Collins were notable contributors in the fiction department and Dickens built up a young staff of regular general contributors such as G. A. Sala, Edmund Yates, and Henry Morley. He himself wrote many of his finest essays for *Household Words*, co-wrote others, and closely monitored all contributions, often revising them extensively, so that the whole journal was stamped with his personality and his views. From the outset the journal was a decided success, achieving in time a stable circulation of 38,500. Particularly popular were the special extra 'Christmas Numbers' (from 1851) which presented multi-authored seasonal stories with a large input from Dickens himself, including each year a different framework for the stories (his own contributions were collected, at first with those of others but later separated out on their own, as *Christmas Stories*).

Late in 1850 Dickens embarked on a project (ultimately unsuccessful) with Edward Bulwer to establish a Guild of Literature and Art to assist impoverished authors and artists. To help raise funds Bulwer wrote a drama, *Not so Bad as we Seem*, which was performed, with Dickens in the leading role, before the queen and Prince Albert (May 1851). 1851 was a difficult year in Dickens's domestic life. Catherine was afflicted by some kind of nervous trouble and Dickens settled her in Malvern with Georgina to try the water cure, visiting her there as often as he could; and there were also two deaths in the family. The first was that of John Dickens, after undergoing an agonizing bladder operation. Dickens was deeply moved by his father's death, and some years later told Forster that the longer he lived, the better man he believed John to have been. The second death was a poignant one, that of his eight-month-old daughter Dora, 'our poor little pet' as he called her (*Letters*, 6.355). Dickens sent Forster to fetch Catherine home from Malvern together with a letter seeking to prepare her as gently as possible for being greeted on arrival with news of the baby's death by saying only that little Dora was very seriously ill and that he did not at all expect her to survive ('why should I say I do, to you my dear!'; ibid., 6.353) . The letter strangely mingles tender concern for Catherine and strong exhortations to her not to abandon herself to grief.

## Social commentaries: *Bleak House* to *Little Dorrit*, 1852–1857

Dickens's increasing anxieties, and anger, about the social and political condition of England during the 1850s—feelings exacerbated by the débâcle of the Crimean War—are evident from a number of fiercely satirical essays that he wrote for *Household Words*, as well as from his intensely anti-aristocratic and anti-monarchical *Child's History of England* serialized in the journal (25 January 1851–10 December 1853). His feelings about public affairs find frequent expression in his letters, for example, when writing to Macready on 4 October 1855:

> what with flunkeyism, toadyism, letting the most contemptible Lords come in for all manner of places ... reading the Court Circular for the New Testament—and bearing such positively awful slaver in the Papers as I saw the other day about a visit of Lord Palmerston's to Woolwich Arsenal—I do reluctantly believe that the English people are, habitually, consenting parties to the miserable imbecility into which we have fallen, *and never will help themselves out of it.* (*Letters*, 7.715–16)

In his only direct intervention in politics (he always steadily refused the invitations he received to stand for parliament) Dickens joined the newly founded Administrative Reform Association and made a scorchingly scornful anti-government speech at its third meeting, on 27 June 1855. But it is above all in the three great novels of this decade—*Bleak House* (published in monthly

parts, 1852–3), *Hard Times* (serialized in *House-*
*hold Words*, 1854), and *Little Dorrit* (monthly
parts, 1855–7)—that his outrage and deep concern about the condition of England most powerfully manifest themselves. The satire of *Bleak
House* focuses on the obfuscations and delays of
the court of chancery which result in widespread
human misery and suffering, but the novel's complicated plot and centripetal organization bring
into the picture a great cross-section of contemporary English society, from the aristocratic Ded-
locks down to Poor Jo, a London crossings-sweeper,
and reveal social injustice, stupidity, muddle, mis-
guided and self-regarding benevolence, charl-
atanism, and gross irresponsibility pervading all
areas of the national life. The court of chancery,
'most pestilent of hoary sinners', serves as the
great emblem of this grim state of affairs. Writing
at the height of his powers, Dickens adopts a virtuoso form of double narration, and the novel has
since the middle of the twentieth century been
widely acclaimed as his greatest work.

*Hard Times*, set in the northern industrial town
of Coketown (usually identified as Preston), is
even more urgently topical (the subtitle appended
when the book appeared in volume form was 'for

these times') and was written, he told Carlyle when asking permission to dedicate the book to him, in the hope that it would 'shake some people in a terrible mistake of these days' (*Letters*, 7.367). 'My satire', he told Charles Knight, 'is against those who see figures and averages, and nothing else—the representatives of the wickedest and most enormous vice of this time' (ibid., 7.492); it is focused on the relentlessly factual, imagination-starving (or warping) educational system favoured by Mr Gradgrind, the embodiment of all that Dickens feared and detested in the theories of political economy and Benthamite utilitarianism. *Little Dorrit*, the saddest of all his novels and also, according to George Bernard Shaw, 'a more seditious book than *Das Kapital*' (*Shaw on Dickens*, 51), brings together scathing criticism of the country's governing institutions (here represented by the all-powerful and all-pervading 'Circumlocution Office'), a vivid portrayal in the story of Mrs Clennam of the harshly Calvinistic version of Christianity that was so strong in Victorian culture, and a depiction of the public greed and gullibility that produces the frenzy of speculation associated with the activity of the swindling financier Mr Merdle, together with Dickens's deeper personal preoccupations about his childhood sufferings and his father's shaming imprisonment in the Marshalsea. Dickens's attack on the inefficiency and ineptitude of the aristo-cratic management of the Royal Literary Fund and his repeated but vain attempts, made with Forster and others, to reform it (1854–8) were another manifestation of his fierce exasperation at this time with the state of contemporary public life.

The later 1850s were also a time of markedly growing tension in Dickens's private life. On the surface things seemed to continue as normal—or, at any rate, as normal for Dickens. In November 1851 he had moved into an eighteen-roomed, porticoed mansion, Tavistock House, in Tavis-tock Square, paying £1524 for a 45-year lease. Catherine bore their tenth and last child, Edward Bulwer Lytton Dickens, in the following year, and the tradition of long family summer holi-days was continued, but now across the channel in Boulogne rather than at Broadstairs. The Dick-enses first visited Boulogne in 1852 and summered there in 1853, 1854, and 1856 (it is described as 'Our French Watering Place' in *Household Words*, 4 November 1854; *Reprinted Pieces*, 1858). But Dickens's growing restlessness was only partly assuaged by such things as his continued zealous labours for Urania Cottage, an autumn (1853) touring holiday in Switzerland and Italy with two younger friends, Wilkie Collins and Augustus Egg, and several rapturously received public readings of the *Christmas Carol* in various provincial towns and cities for the benefit of local charities. He transferred his whole household to Paris for the winter of 1855–6, and in London busied himself with the organization of amateur performances in the schoolroom at Tavistock House of specially written melodramas by Wilkie Collins: *The Lighthouse* in June 1855 and *The Frozen Deep* in January 1857. In the latter play Dickens created a great sensation with his electrifying performance as the brooding hero Richard Wardour who fights his own murderous jealousy, ultimately sacrificing himself to save the life of his successful rival in love. Beneath all this frenetic activity ran an undercurrent of melancholy and gloom seemingly related, at least in part, to a growing dissatisfaction with Catherine. 'Why is it', he wrote to Forster early in 1855, 'that as with poor David [Copperfield], a sense comes always crushing on me now, when I fall into low spirits, as of one happiness I have missed in life, and one friend and companion I have never made?' Later he remarks, 'I find that

the skeleton in my domestic closet is becoming a
pretty big one' (Forster, 638–9).

As if responding to a cue, Maria Beadnell, now
stout Mrs Henry Winter and unseen by Dickens
for at least ten years, chose this moment to get
in touch with him again. Her letter affected him
very powerfully, releasing a flood of passionate
nostalgia for the great love of what he called
his 'hobbledehoyhood'. He wrote her a series of
ardent letters protesting, 'Believe me, you cannot
more tenderly remember our old days and our
old friends than I do', and responding to some
suggestion from her with 'All that you propose, I
accept with my whole heart. Whom can you ever
trust if it be not your old lover!' (*Letters*, 7.533,
544). When they actually met, however, Dickens,
who had arranged matters so that they should be
alone together, was immediately and totally dis-
abused of his wildly romantic idea that the Maria
of their 'old days', long cherished so fondly in his
imagination, was now to be restored to him, and
he quickly retreated into the forms of ordinary
social acquaintance. Dickens the artist proceeded
to make glorious, if somewhat cruel, novelistic
capital out of this serio-comic episode by using the
hapless Mrs Winter as a model for the character of

the hilariously effusive Flora Finching, the hero's old flame in *Little Dorrit*. For Dickens the man, however, the experience must surely have served to intensify his desolating sense of having always, in his emotional life, missed out on something very major, that now yearned-for 'one friendship and companionship' that he felt he had never made (obviously a friendship with a woman, one that combined a sexual charge with intellectual and temperamental compatibility).

# Personal affairs and public career

## Marital breakdown and domestic life

In March 1856 at a cost of £1700 Dickens purchased the pleasant but modest Georgian house
Gad's Hill Place, near Rochester, for use as a
country home. It was a house he had admired on
childhood walks with his father and John Dickens
had told him he might come to own it one day
if he 'were to be very persevering and were to
work hard' (*The Uncommercial Traveller*, 'Travelling Abroad'). This, his 'little Kentish freehold'
as he liked to call it, was the first and only home
that Dickens ever owned, and it was one in which
he took great delight for the rest of his life. He
loved to entertain friends there and was always
devising 'improvements' to the property. At the
time he acquired it, however, his marriage was
well into its last, most intensely unhappy phase.

The situation between him and Catherine was evidently becoming more and more strained. In a letter of 1854 to Miss Burdett-Coutts, Dickens had referred to a 'certain indescribable lassitude of character' in his eldest son that, along with 'tenderer and better qualities', Charley inherited from his mother (*Letters*, 7.245), and it was about this time that 'an unsettled feeling greatly in excess of what was usual with [him]', which Forster claims to have observed in Dickens since 1852, 'became almost habitual' and he failed to find in his home 'the satisfactions which home should have supplied, and which indeed were essential requirements of his nature' (Forster, 635).

It needed only some catalyst to precipitate a catastrophe and such a catalyst soon appeared. Professional actresses were needed to replace Dickens's daughters and Georgina Hogarth for some public performances of *The Frozen Deep* in Manchester in July 1857 (part of the activities organized by Dickens to raise money for the family of the suddenly deceased Douglas Jerrold), and he secured the services of the well-known and highly respected actress Frances Eleanor Ternan (*née* Jarman), and two of her three daughters, Maria and Ellen Lawless Ternan (1839–1914), who were just beginning in the profession. Ellen, always known as Nelly, was eighteen years old, pretty, fair-haired, and intelligent, and Dickens seems to have fallen headlong in love with her. He began very much to concern himself with her affairs and with the fortunes of the Ternan family generally. That autumn, accompanied by Wilkie Collins, he visited Cumberland and made an excursion to Doncaster, where Nelly and Maria were acting. He smuggled ecstatic but veiled references to Nelly into *The Lazy Tour of Two Idle Apprentices*, the account of their northern tour that he and Collins were jointly writing for serialization in *Household Words*. He also included, in one instalment of the *Tour*, a bizarre short story about a man who, weary of his feeble, doting wife, literally wills her to death. Meanwhile, he was writing to Forster:

> Poor Catherine and I are not made for each other and there is no help for it . . . She is exactly what you know, in the way of being amiable and complying; but we are strangely ill-assorted for the bond there is between us. (Forster, 640)

For all her amiability, Catherine would surely have been much disturbed by her husband's sudden intense friendship with a pretty actress who was the same age as their younger daughter, and no doubt Dickens hotly resented this, much as he had earlier resented Catherine's distrust of his peculiar relationship with Mme de la Rue. According to some reports, matters were brought to a head by some jewels intended by Dickens as a present for Nelly being mistakenly delivered to Catherine instead.

By the following spring Dickens, not content with having moved into a separate bedroom and having had the communicating door between it and his wife's room boarded up, had decided that he must have a legal separation from her and drove the arrangements for this ruthlessly forward. Infuriated by the rumours (no doubt about his relations with Nelly) being spread, apparently by Catherine's mother and her sister Helen, he insisted on their signing a retraction and also took the extraordinary step of publishing a statement about his domestic affairs in *The Times* (7 June 1858) and in other papers, including his own *Household Words* (12 June), imprudently asserting the innocence of a certain young lady unspecified. Scandal had been given further food to chew on when it had become known that Georgina

Hogarth had chosen to stay with Dickens while Catherine, with only her eldest son for company and an income of £600 per annum, was resettled in a house in north-west London, and it may well have been his sister-in-law's reputation that Dickens was primarily seeking to protect. There then appeared in the English press, copied from the New York *Tribune* of 16 August 1858, a private letter about the separation written by Dickens to Arthur Smith, manager of his public readings, in which he asserted that Catherine had no real love for her children, nor they for her, and hinted that she suffered from some mental instability. Dickens always strongly protested that this letter had never been intended for publication and referred to it as 'the violated letter', but his continued affectionate friendship for Smith (whom he had commissioned to show the letter 'to anyone who wishes to do him [Dickens] right') suggests that he cannot have been all that sorry that the letter had become public, and may even have connived at this. It was about this time that his attitude to Catherine suddenly changed to one of implacable hostility. She had, he told Miss Burdett-Coutts who was seeking to mediate between him and Catherine, caused him 'unspeakable agony of mind' and he wanted 'to communicate with her no more'

(*Letters*, 7.632). During the remaining twelve years of his life he wrote to her only three times, each time merely a terse response to a communication from her.

Before the end of 1859 the pattern of Dickens's domestic and personal life for the remainder of his days was firmly set. Georgina Hogarth, helped by his adoring elder daughter Mary (Mamie), who never married, managed the household at Gad's Hill, to his entire and frequently-expressed satisfaction. Georgina devoted herself primarily to the comfort and well-being of her illustrious brother-in-law and secondarily to the welfare of his younger sons, each of whom was early launched into the world, only one of them, Henry, being sent to university (Cambridge). Katey, Dickens's highly spirited and much loved younger daughter, married the artist Charles Collins, brother of Wilkie, in 1860, simply because, according to Gladys Storey, an intimate friend of her later years, she was eager to leave home after her mother's banishment (Katey is quoted as saying 'My father was like a madman when my mother left home.... He did not care a damn what happened to any of us'; Storey, 96).

Mrs Ternan and her daughters settled in a substantial family house in Houghton Place, north-west London. The lease was, almost certainly, purchased for Nelly by Dickens in the name of her sisters Fanny and Maria in 1859; she took over the lease from them when she came of age the following year and retained it until 1901. She and her mother later lived in a cottage in Slough and then a house in Peckham, the rates in both places being paid by a 'Mr Tringham', generally assumed to have been Dickens. After he had sold the lease of Tavistock House in 1860, Gad's Hill was, as far as the public knew, Dickens's only domestic base. There is evidence, however, that he regularly visited Nelly in Houghton Place, as well as in Slough and Peckham, also that he spent time in France with her during the 1860s, staying in a small house in Condette, near Boulogne, that belonged to his former Boulogne landlord, M. Beaucourt-Mutuel (the lovingly portrayed 'M. Loyal Devasseur' of 'Our French Watering Place', *Reprinted Pieces*, 1858). The precise nature and history of their relationship—whether, for example, she—sooner or later—became his mistress, as most biographers now assume, or whether his passion remained, for whatever reason, unconsummated—remains a matter of debate. Storey was apparently told by Sir Henry Dickens in 1928 that Nelly had a son with Dickens but that the child died very young (Slater, 379; Storey, 94); no hard evidence for the existence of this ill-fated putative infant has so far come to light.

One of the non-domestic casualties of Dickens's break with his wife was his friendship with William Thackeray. The two men had known each other since 1836, when Thackeray had unsuccessfully proposed himself as a replacement illustrator for *Pickwick Papers* following Seymour's suicide. They had been on friendly and sociable terms but never intimate, and found themselves on opposing sides in the so-called 'dignity of literature debate' (Dickens in his obituary of Thackeray in *The Cornhill*, February 1864, said he thought his fellow novelist 'too much feigned a want of earnestness' in his profession). After the great success of *Vanity Fair* (1847–8) Thackeray was seen by many as challenging Dickens's novelistic pre-eminence, even though his sales never remotely approached those of Dickens's books; injudicious admirers on both sides tended to praise one writer at the expense of the other. When Thackeray heard gossip at his club blaming the break-up of Dickens's marriage on an intrigue with Georgina Hogarth, he said, 'no such thing—its with an actress' (*The Letters and Private Papers of William Makepeace Thackeray*, ed., G. N. Ray, 4 vols, 1945–6, 4.86). This, but not the original rumour, was reported to Dickens, enraging him. This rage no doubt lay behind his energetic championship of one of his 'young men', Edmund Yates, in the celebrated 'Garrick Club affair' of 1858. Thackeray demanded Yates's expulsion from the club for publishing a hostile account of Thackeray's conversational manner which he could have observed only at the Garrick and Yates was duly expelled. Dickens, who had intervened on Yates's behalf, angrily resigned from the club in protest and he and Thackeray ceased to be on speaking terms. There was no reconciliation until they chanced to meet each other at another club, the Athenaeum, late in 1863, just a few weeks before Thackeray's sudden death.

## A new career: the public readings, 1858–1867

By 1858 Dickens had many times exploited his considerable histrionic talents in giving enormously successful public readings of the *Carol* and *The Cricket on the Hearth* for charity, and he had long been under pressure to accept invitations to read for money. It was doubtless the combination, in the late 1850s, of his extreme restlessness and his need for increased income after buying Gad's Hill that persuaded him to embark on a series of paid weekly readings during the 1858 London season. This was much against advice from Forster, who considered it undignified for a great writer to present himself to the public as a paid performer, even of his own works. The first series of readings began on 29 April and the tremendous warmth of the audiences' response would certainly have reassured Dickens that he had not been at all damaged, in the eyes of his adoring readers, by the recent upheaval in his domestic life. He went on to tour a number of provincial English cities, as well as Edinburgh, Glasgow, Belfast, and Dublin, with a repertory expanded to include items drawn from *Pickwick* (the Bardell trial), *Chuzzlewit* (a piece centred on Mrs Gamp), and *Dombey* (*The Story of Little Dombey*), as well as from various of the 'Christmas Stories' published in *Household Words*. In Arthur Smith he had an efficient and highly congenial manager, on whom he could rely completely, and he had a full support crew as well. He stood behind a specially designed reading-desk, brilliantly illuminated by gaslights. Each item had been carefully prepared and intensively rehearsed so that he knew the texts by heart, *performed* them rather than read them, and could introduce spontaneous variations in response to the reaction of a particular audience. 'He does not only *read* his story; he *acts* it', wrote one reviewer, 'Each character . . . is as completely assumed and individualised . . . as though he was personating it in costume on the stage' (Collins, *Readings*, lix). Everywhere he met with triumphant success and tremendous enthusiasm on the part of his overflowing audiences. The American writer Moncure D. Conway commented that at the end of one of his readings 'it was not mere applause that followed, but a passionate outburst of love for the man' (ibid., xxii). It was striking, and no doubt deeply gratifying, evidence for his belief that his relationship with the British public was a very 'particular' one—'personally affectionate and like no other man's' (Forster, 646).

Other provincial tours followed in the autumn of 1859 and in the autumn and winter of 1861–2 with more items added to the repertory, including a sensational *Copperfield* reading which became a favourite with both Dickens and his audiences (though the top favourites always remained the Bardell trial from *Pickwick* and the *Carol*). Arthur Smith's untimely death in 1861 was a severe blow and Dickens gave only two short seasons of readings in London in 1862 and 1863 (there were also three very well-received 'charity' readings at the British embassy in Paris in January 1863). He had found it a strain to perform while also continuing to write a novel (*Great Expectations*) so there were no more readings during the time he was writing *Our Mutual Friend* (spring 1864–winter 1865). But in 1866 he contracted with the music publishers and concert promoters Chappell & Co. for a series of thirty readings in London and elsewhere. Chappell undertook all the business side of the performances and paid Dickens a fee of £50 per night (which by 1870 had risen to £80 per night); the firm also appointed a manager for the readings, George Dolby, who became a trusted friend and confidant of his 'Chief' as he called Dickens. Another tour of England and Ireland took place during January–May 1867, preparatory to taking the readings to America.

## All the Year Round, *A Tale of Two Cities,* and *Great Expectations,* 1859–1861

When, in 1859, Dickens decided to publish a statement in the press about his personal affairs he expected that Bradbury and Evans would run it in *Punch*, which they also published. He was furious when they, very reasonably, declined to insert 'statements on a domestic and painful subject in the inappropriate columns of a comic miscellany' (Patten, 262). He therefore determined to break with them completely and to return to his old publishers Chapman and Hall. Bradbury and Evans's co-operation was needed, however, for the launch of the elegant Library Edition of Dickens's works (twenty-two volumes published, 1858–9; re-issued with illustrations and eight more volumes, 1861–74). But Dickens forced the dissolution of *Household Words*, owned jointly by himself and Bradbury and Evans, and the last number appeared, despite all the hapless publishers' efforts to prevent the closure, on 28 May 1859. Dickens, meanwhile, had begun publishing, from 30 April, a new weekly periodical with the same format and at the same price as *Household Words* called *All the Year Round*. Wills continued as his sub-editor and he and Dickens were the sole proprietors,

Dickens owning 75 per cent of the shares as well as the name and goodwill attached to the magazine. While maintaining the tradition of anonymity for all non-fictional contributions, *All the Year Round* differed from its predecessor in various ways, not least in its greater emphasis on serialized fiction. A new instalment of the current serial stood always first in each weekly number, and Dickens editorially proclaimed 'it is our hope and aim [that the stories so serialized in the journal] may become a part of English literature' (*All the Year Round*, 2.95).

Dickens himself inaugurated the series in spectacularly successful fashion with his second historical novel, *A Tale of Two Cities* (serialized from 30 April to 26 November 1859), the basic plot of which was inspired by the story of the self-sacrificing lover Richard Wardour (Dickens's role) in *The Frozen Deep*. In this novel, the second half of which takes place during the French Revolution, Dickens set himself the task, he told Forster, 'of making *a picturesque story*, rising in every chapter with characters true to nature, but whom the story itself should express, more than they should express themselves, by dialogue', glossed by Forster as meaning that Dickens would be

relying 'less upon character than upon incident'
(Forster, 730, 731). In its tightly organized and
highly romantic melodrama and the near-absence
of typical 'Dickensian' humour and humorous
characters, *A Tale of Two Cities* certainly stands
apart from all his other novels, although—as in
his earlier historical novel—one of the great set
pieces of the book is the anarchic destruction of
a prison, an event to which Dickens's imagination responded with powerful ambiguity. Thanks
partly to this new Dickens story, and partly to
a vigorous advertising campaign organized by
Wills, *All the Year Round* had an initial circulation of 120,000. Wilkie Collins's sensationally
popular 'sensation novel' *The Woman in White*
followed *A Tale of Two Cities* in the serial slot,
contributing not a little to the maintenance of the
magazine's impressive circulation figures. These
eventually settled down to a steady 100,000 with
an occasional dip but soaring always (up as far as
300,000) for the special 'extra Christmas Numbers'. Dickens eventually wearied of this latter
feature, however, and killed it off after 1867.

Compared with *Household Words*, *All the Year
Round* features far fewer journalistic pieces by
Dickens himself, the 'Uncommercial Traveller'

essays (see below) notwithstanding, and it has a much greater focus on topics of foreign interest, notably the struggle for Italian unification, and much less concern for the political and social condition of England than the earlier magazine. Nor could it be quite so topical as *Household Words* since every issue had to be finalized a fortnight before its due publication date, Dickens having contracted with the New York publishers J. M. Emerson & Co. to send them stereotype plates of every issue in order to ensure its simultaneous appearance on both sides of the Atlantic (an arrangement later somewhat modified).

On 28 January 1860 Dickens began contributing to his new journal a series of occasional essays in the character of 'the Uncommercial Traveller'. They were discontinued when he began work in earnest on *Great Expectations* (1 December 1860– 3 August 1861) and not resumed until 2 May 1863 (carrying on until 24 October 1863). The 'Uncommercial Traveller' essays, which feature some of the finest prose ever written by Dickens, take sometimes a quasi-autobiographical form, with reminiscences of childhood, like 'Nurse's Stories' or 'Dullborough Town' (that is, Rochester), and are sometimes examples of superb investigative reporting, notably of lesser-known aspects of life in London; yet others focus on the process of travel itself, in its many various forms.

As for his fictional writing, Dickens had intended his next novel to be published in the old twenty-monthly-number 'green-leaved' format but changed plans when Charles Lever's *A Day's Ride*, which followed *The Woman in White*, failed to hold readers' interest and caused a perceptible drop in the circulation figures. Dickens assured Forster that 'The property of *All the Year Round*' was 'far too valuable, in every way, to be much endangered' by this development (Forster, 733); nevertheless he was determined to take no risks and so 'struck in' with his new story, *Great Expectations*, the second of his novels to be written wholly in the first person, now replanned as a weekly serial. The circulation figures promptly recovered and in this chance way (at least, as regards its format) there came into being the story that for many critics (and for many 'common readers' too) represents the very highest reach of Dickens's art as a novelist—even with the revised ending that Edward Bulwer Lytton persuaded him to write in order to avoid too starkly sad a conclusion to this masterfully structured and brilliantly written story of money, class, sex, and obsessive mental states with, for the first time ever in Dickens's major fiction, a protagonist who is unambiguously working-class. The novel was published in three volumes unillustrated, Dickens probably recognizing that Browne's style had not really kept pace with the development of his own novelistic art, as was evidenced by the feebleness of the illustrations Browne supplied for the volume edition of *A Tale of Two Cities*.

## *Our Mutual Friend* and the Staplehurst railway disaster, 1861–1865

The gestation of Dickens's last completed novel was 'unusually prolonged and frustrating' (Schlicke, 434). For at least three years before mid-January 1864 when he was at last able to report to Forster that he had actually begun writing, he had been struggling to get started, turning over notions for situations and characters jotted down in a book of memoranda that he had been keeping for some time (ed. Kaplan, published New York Public Library, 1981); many of these notions were used in the novel as it finally took shape. Two family deaths occurred in 1863. The first was that of Dickens's second son, Walter, who died in India, and the second that of his mother. Dickens grieved for his son (but, bleakly, did not communicate with Catherine, who must have been quite as grief-stricken) but it is not difficult to sense a continuing hardness of attitude towards his mother as she sank gradually into increasing senility. He wrote in a grimly comic vein to a woman friend of how

the impossibility of getting her [his mother] to understand what is the matter, combined with her desire to be got up in sables like a female Hamlet, illumines the dreary scene with a ghastly absurdity that is the chief relief I can find in it. (*Letters*, 9.287)

For *Our Mutual Friend* he reverted to his traditional form of publication in twenty monthly numbers (May 1864–December 1865) and at first felt 'quite dazed', he told Wilkie Collins, by the return to 'the large canvas and the big brushes' (ibid., 10.346). The illustrator chosen for the work was the orphaned son of an old artist friend, young Marcus Stone, who worked in the sentimental-realist style of 1860s book illustration, quite different from the caricatural style of Cruikshank and Browne.

The novel with its panoramic treatment of contemporary society, complex plotting, scathing social satire, and masterly emblematic art recalls both *Bleak House* and *Little Dorrit*. It differs from these predecessors in a number of important ways, however. Most notably, both of the love stories at the heart of the book (the earlier novels each have only one main love story) end on a very positive note, neither involving retreat from the city as in the case of Esther and Alan Woodcourt in *Bleak House*, nor yielding themselves up to it as in the case of Little Dorrit and Arthur Clennam in *Dorrit*. *Our Mutual Friend* had a mixed reception (the young Henry James's harshly dismissive review in *The Nation* is notorious) but its stock has risen dramatically in recent years and it is now generally regarded as one of his very greatest works. While writing it Dickens, travelling back from France with Nelly Ternan and her mother, was involved in a serious railway accident at Staplehurst on 9 June 1865, in which ten people died. Dickens himself was unhurt but very badly shaken, not only by the accident itself but also by the experience of working for hours afterwards among the injured and the dying and trying to alleviate their sufferings, mainly by administering brandy to them from the bottle and a half which 'by an extraordinary chance' he happened to have with him (ibid., 11.61). Nelly seems to have been among those who were only slightly injured and presumably she and her mother were got away to London as quickly as possible. She is often referred to as 'the Patient' in Dickens's letters thereafter.

## Return to America, 1867–1868

From the outset of his public readings career Dickens had been contemplating the possibility of an American tour, but he dreaded the long separation from Nelly and then the outbreak of the civil war put the whole idea out of the question. By May 1867, however, the attractions of America as what he had once called 'a golden campaigning ground' (*Letters*, 5.396) had become very strong indeed in the face of his ever-increasing expenses; he wrote that he began to feel himself 'drawn to America, as Darnay in *A Tale of Two Cities* was attracted to the Loadstone Rock, Paris' (Forster, 707). Dickens appointed George Dolby as his tour manager and sent him across the Atlantic on a reconnaissance expedition and, after receiving a favourable report and being fêted at a grand farewell banquet, himself left for the States.

The tour began in Boston on 2 December 1867 and ended in New York on 20 April 1868, two days before he sailed for home aboard the *Russia*. Harsh weather, a punishing schedule, and the often enormous American auditoria made the tour a severe ordeal for Dickens who was suffering from 'a truly American catarrh' and exhaustion, as well as from lameness resulting from 'a neuralgic affection of the right foot', aggravated by his insistence on walking long distances in deep snow whenever possible. He seems to have nourished a hope that Nelly might come to America (she had cousins in Newburyport, Massachusetts, and perhaps considered visiting them) but this was soon given up, and he had to content himself with sending her letters via Wills with covering messages such as 'Another letter for my Darling enclosed' (*Letters*, 11.528). He did, however, receive most devoted support and tender care from Dolby, and also from his American publisher James T. Fields and Fields's charming wife, Annie. Dickens and Annie clearly shared a strong bond of mutual affection, and she seems to have been sensitive to the pain and trouble that lay beneath his sparkling public persona ('it is wonderful', she wrote in her journal, 'the fun and flow of spirits C.D. has for he is a sad man';

Curry, 44). Despite constant troubles with ticket touts and continued hostility from some sections of Dickens's old enemy, the American press, the tour was a most triumphant success (neither sickness nor exhaustion ever prevented Dickens from turning in a great performance at the reading-desk) and netted him over £19,000, a sum which might have been much greater if he had not in his distrust of American currency insisted on changing his dollars into gold at a 40 per cent discount.

## Last years and *Edwin Drood*, 1868–1870

While in America, Dickens published in the *Atlantic Monthly* (January–March 1868) a hauntingly strange first-person narrative, 'George Silverman's Explanation', which has yielded rich food for biographical criticism, and in *Our Young Folks* (January and March–May 1868) 'Holiday Romance', four stories for children purportedly written by children. All these stories also appeared in *All the Year Round*. Back in England and recuperating from the strenuous tour, he postponed starting a new novel and concentrated on planning a long farewell tour partly in London and partly in the provinces. This began in London on 6 October 1868. Now included in Dickens's repertory was a highly sensational new reading derived from *Oliver Twist* (the murder of Nancy), the performance of which became almost an obsession with him despite warnings by doctors and friends that it was adversely affecting his health. In fact, by late April 1869 he had become so unwell that his doctors ordered him to abandon the tour. Anxious to compensate Chappells for the loss they had sustained, he prevailed on his doctor to allow him to present a final series of twelve readings in London (January–March 1870). He famously ended the last of these by saying, 'From these garish lights I vanish now for evermore with a heartfelt, grateful, respectful and affectionate farewell' (*Speeches*, ed. Fielding, 413). On 9 March he was received in audience by Queen Victoria, who recorded that he 'talked of the division of classes in England which he hoped would get better in time. He felt sure it would come gradually' (*Letters of Queen Victoria*, ed. G. E. Buckle, 2nd ser., 1926–8, 2). On 5 April Dickens presided in sparkling form, as he had done many times before, at the annual dinner of the Newsvendors' Benevolent Institution and on 30 April replied to the toast to 'literature' at the Royal Academy banquet, paying an eloquent and heartfelt tribute to his old friend Daniel Maclise whose sudden death just a few days before had greatly shaken him.

In April also there appeared the first instalment of Dickens's new novel, *The Mystery of Edwin Drood*, set mainly in Rochester ('Cloisterham') and planned for publication in eleven monthly instalments, the last one to be a double number. It was to be a murder story, 'the originality of which was to consist in the review of the murderer's career by himself at the close, when its temptations were to be dwelt upon as if, not he the culprit, but some other man were the tempted' (Forster, 808). It was the culmination of Dickens's lifelong fascination with the demeanour and psychology of murderers and he was, his daughter Katey remembered, 'quite as deeply fascinated and absorbed in the study of the criminal Jasper as in the dark and sinister crime that has given the book its title' (' "Edwin Drood" and the last days of Charles Dickens', *Pall Mall Magazine*, June 1906, 644). *Drood* was very favourably received, selling 10,000 more copies than *Our Mutual Friend* and showing in its descriptive passages, Forster believed, that Dickens's 'imaginative power was at its best' (Forster, 808). The story was to have been illustrated by Katey's husband, Charles Collins, but ill health compelled him to withdraw after designing the monthly-part cover and he was replaced by Luke Fildes.

Dickens lived long enough to complete only six numbers of the novel, and soon a whole *Drood* 'industry' (which still flourishes today) grew up, concerned with providing a plausible solution to the mystery. Dickens was working on *Drood* in his little Swiss chalet (the gift of his actor friend Charles Fechter) in the garden at Gad's Hill on the morning of 8 June 1870, the day on which he later suffered a stroke from which he died the following day. An alternative oral tradition about how Dickens died is quoted by Claire Tomalin to her *Invisible Woman* (new edn, 1991). According to this account, he suffered his stroke while visiting Nelly in Peckham and was taken, in an unconscious state, by her in a closed cab to Gad's Hill where she delivered him into Georgina's care. His wish to be buried 'in the small graveyard under Rochester Castle wall' (Forster, 855) was overridden by a national demand that he should rest in Westminster Abbey where he was accordingly buried on 14 June, in the strictly private ceremony that he had so forcefully enjoined in his will.

Dickens was survived by his repudiated wife for nine years, during which time Catherine preserved, in public at least, a dignified silence about their marital history, though she did when dying ask her younger daughter to give her collection of letters from Dickens to the British Museum, 'that the world may know he loved me once' (Storey, 164). Dickens was also survived by eight of his children. His eldest son, Charley, died leaving seven children in 1896, the same year as Mamie who died unmarried. Katey, who had some success as a painter, exhibiting regularly at the Royal Academy, had one son with her second husband, another artist, Carlo Perugini, but the child died in infancy and Katey herself died in 1929. Francis died childless in America in 1886, after serving for twelve years in Canada with the North-West Mounted Police. Alfred emigrated to Australia, married twice, and in 1910 returned to England to begin a successful career lecturing on his father and his books, dying suddenly in New York in 1912, survived by two daughters from his first marriage (both of whom died unmarried). Sydney, a naval cadet, died at sea in 1872, leaving no children; Henry became a High Court judge and a knight of the realm and died, leaving children, in 1933; and Edward (always known as Plorn), who married and became a member of the parliament of New South Wales, died in Australia childless in 1902. The numerous direct descendants of Dickens alive today all trace their descent from their illustrious ancestor either through Charley's line or through Henry's.

# Reputation and legacy

## Dickens's after-fame

From a very early period of Dickens's career many of his great comic and/or grotesque characters took on a life of their own in the culture (both high and low) of the English-speaking world and have ever since been recognized and referred to by people who may well have never read a single Dickens novel. This resulted from his extraordinary ability to create, and give unforgettably expressive names to, figures who are highly individualized by their physical appearance, dress, and mannerisms, and who are also powerfully allegorical, being brilliant incarnations of various aspects of perennial human nature. Mr Pickwick and Sam Weller, Oliver Twist asking for more, the Artful Dodger, Fagin, Sikes and the murder of Nancy, the death of Little Nell, Scrooge and

Tiny Tim, Mr Pecksniff, Mrs Gamp, Uriah Heep, Mr Micawber hourly expecting something to turn up and Mrs Micawber refusing to desert him— these are some of the main Dickens characters and scenes that have been, and continue to be, drawn on over and over again by advertisers, illustrators, cartoonists, journalists, politicians, and public speakers generally throughout the English-speaking world to point a moral or adorn a tale, to satirize or to celebrate some contemporary figure or state of affairs.

After Shakespeare, Dickens is probably the most quoted writer in English and, indeed, the names of certain characters, Bumble and Scrooge, for instance, have become part of the language itself. The same is true of the adjective 'Dickensian' which, depending on the context, is used to mean one of three things: festive or jolly (a Dickensian Christmas, for example); squalid or antiquated (as in 'a Dickensian slum' or 'to work in positively Dickensian conditions'); or characters so idiosyncratic and improbable as to seem to belong in a Dickens novel ('a truly Dickensian waiter').

The general concept of Victorian London derives in great measure from Dickens's elaborate,

haunting descriptions of labyrinthine courts and
alleyways, quaint old buildings, fogs, gaslight,
and teeming street life; and tourists still come
to the capital from all over the world eager to
discover and experience 'Dickens's London'. Nor
is such topographical enthusiasm confined to the
capital. 'Dickens's England' in general has also
always been attractive to tourists, strongly drawn
as they are to places closely associated with either
his life or his books; an early classic of this
kind of tourism was William Hughes's *A Week's
Tramp in Dickens-Land* (1891). Pre-eminent in
this respect are the Kentish towns of Broadstairs
and Rochester, both of which have for many
years held an annual 'Dickens festival', Rochester
having the additional advantage of proximity to
Gad's Hill Place and to 'the *Great Expectations*
country' of the Kentish marshes.

At his death Dickens was regarded by the great
mass of his contemporaries not simply as a great
writer but also as a great and good man, a
champion of the poor and downtrodden, who
had striven hard throughout his whole career for
greater social justice and a better, kinder world.
It was this perception of him as much as relish
for his literary art that inspired the founding

of the international Dickens Fellowship in 1902, intended, according to its stated aims and objects, to 'knit together in a common bond of friendship lovers of the great master of humour and pathos, Charles Dickens', to spread the love of humanity ('the keynote of all his work'), to campaign against those 'social evils' which would most have concerned him, and to help preserve buildings and objects associated with him. This organization still flourishes today and still engages in charitable work, though it now approximates more closely to a conventional literary society. It has over forty autonomous branches throughout the English-speaking world (with, currently, others in France, Holland, and Japan), it elects the majority of the board of trustees governing the Charles Dickens Museum at 48 Doughty Street, London (which it saved from threatened demolition in 1923 and opened to the public two years later), and since 1905 it has published a journal called *The Dickensian*, devoted to the study and discussion of all aspects of Dickens's life, work, and reputation and the monitoring of his public image.

The perception of Dickens as a great good man underwent a marked change after 1934 when the first revelations about his relationship with Nelly

Ternan were published in the *Daily Express* by the biographer and literary antiquary Thomas Wright (Nelly herself had quietly married six years after Dickens's death, had become the mother of two children, and had died in 1914). The continuing fascination with Dickens's connection with her (every twenty or thirty years a new book about it appears, and it is constantly being excitedly rediscovered by the media) attests to the unique position occupied by Dickens in contemporary Anglo-American culture. Despite his broken marriage and the periodic re-investigations of the Ternan affair, he is still very much an icon of those traditional domestic and social virtues often assumed to have been part of 'Victorian values', his universally recognizable image as a bearded great Victorian having appeared for several years on British £10 notes; and he is forever inextricably associated with Christmas cheer and seasonal charitable feelings.

For some seventy years following Dickens's death there was a marked gap between his enormous and unfailing popularity with ordinary readers and the attitude towards him of the highly cultured, including members of the academic world. As George Ford showed in his *Dickens and his*

*Readers* (1955), admirers of George Eliot and George Meredith tended to dismiss Dickens as 'vulgar' and lacking in artistic merit, an attitude that persisted into the Bloomsbury-dominated criticism of the 1920s and 1930s. Writing on Dickens in the first *Dictionary of National Biography* (1888), Sir Leslie Stephen commented: 'If literary fame could safely be measured by popularity with the half-educated, Dickens must claim the highest position among English novelists', and Aldous Huxley made Dickens and the death of Little Nell his prime example in his *Vulgarity in Literature* (1930).

Dickens and his art did, however, have a magnificent champion during the early decades of the last century in the bulky shape of G. K. Chesterton, now generally acknowledged to be the greatest Dickens critic of all time. It was not until the American cultural critic Edmund Wilson, responding to the Ternan revelations and invoking Freudian theory, argued for a much more complex interpretation of Dickens's personality and art in his seminal essay 'Dickens: the two Scrooges' (in *The Wound and the Bow: Seven Studies in Literature*, 1941), that a truly seismic shift began in high-cultural and academic attitudes towards Dickens. Where Chesterton had celebrated above all the comic splendours of the earlier Dickens novels, Wilson directed readers' attention towards the later, 'darker' works. Important studies by George Orwell (in his *Inside the Whale*, 1940) and Humphry House (*The Dickens World*, 1941) further encouraged a total and wide-ranging revaluation of Dickens by literary critics and academic professionals, as did the first full-scale scholarly biography by Edgar Johnson (1952), the pioneering textual work of John Butt and Kathleen Tillotson (*Dickens at Work*, 1957), and the American literary scholar J. Hillis Miller's hugely influential *Charles Dickens: the World of his Novels* (1958), a rereading of many of the novels in the light of the phenomenological theory of Georges Poulet. Even F. R. Leavis, who in 1948 had, very magisterially and influentially, excluded all Dickens, apart from *Hard Times*, from 'the great tradition' of the English novel, underwent a conversion and in *Dickens the Novelist* (1970) joined forces with his wife, Q. D. Leavis, to praise him as one of the greatest writers of all time.

From the second half of the twentieth century Dickens has been, and continues to be, the subject of innumerable academic treatises and conferences (including an annual week-long gathering at the 'Dickens Universe' in the University of California at Santa Cruz). A never-ending stream of editions of his novels has poured from the press, alongside books and scholarly articles investigating and variously interpreting all aspects of his life and work, and major scholarly editions of his speeches, letters, and journalism. The Dickens Society of America (founded 1970) publishes the *Dickens Quarterly*, originally the *Dickens Studies Newsletter*. Once again, the only comparison is with the great proliferation of all branches of Shakespeare studies in recent decades. Meanwhile, Dickens continues to be widely read by non-academic readers, many of them nowadays perhaps turning to his books for the first time as a result of seeing film or television adaptations.

## Dickens on stage, screen, and air

From the time of *The Pickwick Papers* onwards, Dickens found his phenomenal popularity being extensively exploited, with complete immunity under the law, by theatrical hack writers such as William Moncrieff and Edward Stirling who produced (often very crude) dramatized versions of his books for the London theatres. Such versions were frequently staged with clumsily inept endings even before Dickens had finished writing his novel. They provided splendid roles for star actors, like W. J. Hammond whose Sam Weller in Moncrieff's *The Pickwickians* (1837) was hugely popular, or Richard [O.] Smith who played Scrooge in Stirling's *A Christmas Carol* (1844), and they generally drew large audiences so were popular with both actors and managers. No fewer than seventeen different adaptations of *The Cricket on the Hearth* appeared on the London stage within a month of the book's publication (December 1845). Although, as Philip Bolton shows, the spate of Dickens dramatizations diminished somewhat after the mid-century, his 1987 work *Dickens Dramatised* is nevertheless able to list some 3000 dramatic adaptations of the novelist's work for stage, screen, and radio, at the same time acknowledging that this must be a very incomplete reckoning. For there has never been a period when Dickens's work has ceased to interest dramatizers and actors. Jennie Lee, a Victorian actress, made a whole career out of playing the title-role in her husband J. P. Burnett's *Jo, or, Bleak House* (first produced in 1876), and Sir John Martin-Harvey played Sidney Carton for over forty years in a hugely successful adaptation of *A Tale of Two Cities* called *The Only Way* (first produced 1899). The music-hall artist Bransby Williams, who was celebrated from 1896 onwards for his impersonations of Dickens characters, lived long enough to perform them on radio and even television. In 1951 Emlyn Williams impersonated Dickens himself in a one-man show based on Dickens's public readings. This proved enormously popular all over the world and he continued to present it until he died nearly forty years later. More recent successes in this line have been Patrick Stewart's one-man performance of *A Christmas Carol* in London during the 1993–4 Christmas season, and Simon Callow's *The Mystery of Charles Dickens*, scripted by Peter Ackroyd, author of a widely-acclaimed biography of Dickens, at the Albery Theatre, London, in 2000–01. Both these productions were indebted to Dickens's public readings style. Stewart actually used a reading-desk similar to that used by Dickens himself, and Callow had earlier performed several of Dickens's reading texts on BBC television before a studio audience. Highly successful also was Miriam Margolyes's one-woman show *Dickens's Women* (1991, Duke of York's Theatre, London) in which Margolyes introduced and performed a remarkable

range of Dickens's female characters. At the other
end of the theatrical spectrum from one-man
shows, Lionel Bart's *Oliver!*, first produced in 1960,
very frequently revived, and brilliantly filmed by
Carol Reed in 1968, must be regarded as one
of the most successful musicals of all time. The
Royal Shakespeare Company's tremendously popular epic production in 1982 of an eight-hour
version of *Nicholas Nickleby*, scripted by David
Edgar and with thirty-nine people in the cast, was
another landmark in the history of Dickens on
stage.

Dickens was a great standby of the early film
industry and a profound influence on the legen-
dary Hollywood director D. W. Griffith, as famously discussed in Sergei Eisenstein's 'Dickens,
Griffith and the film today' (in *Film Form: Essays
in Film Theory*, 1949). A number of silent films
were made of Dickens's novels, notably by the
British film-maker Thomas Bentley in the second
decade of the twentieth century. The arrival of
the talkies reproduced the situation created by
the nineteenth-century theatre with many cine-
matic versions of Dickens's novels built around
star actors: MGM's *David Copperfield* (1934),
for example, starring W. C. Fields as Micawber,

and the same studio's *A Tale of Two Cities* (1935) starring Ronald Colman as Sydney Carton; Paramount's *A Christmas Carol* (1935) starring Sir Seymour Hicks as Scrooge; and, in Britain, Renown's *A Christmas Carol* (1951) starring Alastair Sim as Scrooge and J. Arthur Rank's *A Tale of Two Cities* (1958) starring Dirk Bogarde as Sydney Carton. Since the Second World War dozens of Dickens films have been made in Britain and America; two, directed by David Lean, stand out as real masterpieces: *Great Expectations* (1946) and *Oliver Twist* (1947). The latter is not simply a vehicle for star actors (though it has a superb cast), but a totally successful, highly imaginative translation of Dickens's novel into another medium, as is also the Portuguese director João Botelho's striking screen version of *Hard Times* (*Tempos difíceis, este tempo*, 1988), set in contemporary Portugal and filmed in black and white. Compared with the rarity of successful stage or film versions of Dickens's novels, there have been, since the 1940s, scores of very good radio and television serializations of the books, mainly on the BBC, something that should come as no surprise given that the stories were themselves originally conceived of as serials and published in this form. Outstanding among more recent adaptations have been *Bleak House* (1985), scripted by Arthur Hopcraft, *Martin Chuzzlewit* (1994), by David Lodge, and *Our Mutual Friend* (1998), by Sandy Welch.

## Dickens's impact on world literature

There can be few other English writers—apart, of course, from Shakespeare—with such widespread influence as Dickens, not only on their successors in the national literature, but also on major foreign writers, and few have been the subject of so many outstanding treatises by foreign critics. George Gissing, George Bernard Shaw, H. G. Wells, Joseph Conrad, James Joyce— these are among the most distinguished of late nineteenth-century and early twentieth-century writers whose work shows clear signs of Dickens's influence without any of the slavish imitativeness shown by the great tribe of avowedly 'Dickensian' writers like William De Morgan. Gissing also wrote some outstandingly good criticism of Dickens. The most celebrated examples of great foreign writers profoundly influenced by Dickens are Dostoyevsky (in his 'Two Scrooges' essay Edmund Wilson noted the irony that 'The Bloomsbury that talked about Dostoevsky ignored

Dostoevsky's master, Dickens') and Franz Kafka. The intense and abiding admiration felt for Dickens by Turgenev and Tolstoy is also well documented. And, as Ada Nisbet amply demonstrated in her Dickens chapter in Lionel Stevenson's *Victorian Fiction: a Guide to Research* (1964), the presence of Dickens has been clearly traced in writers as various, and from as varied backgrounds, as Hans Christian Andersen, William Faulkner, Proust, Fontane, Benito Galdos, and Strindberg, and a number of communist Chinese authors. The great Japanese novelist Soseki Natsume (1867–1916) is another outstanding example she might have cited. Nisbet also surveys the wealth of foreign (non-English-speaking) critical response to Dickens, with important and substantial studies by critics as distinguished as Hippolyte Taine, Wilhelm Dibelius, Stefan Zweig, and Mario Praz. And today there exists, as has been indicated above, a mighty international academic industry centred on Dickens, demonstrating, in a way that the gasman who accompanied Dickens on his readings tours could hardly have imagined, the truth of his fervent praise of his great 'Chief': 'The more you want out of the Master, the more you will get out of him.'

# *Sources*

J. Forster, *The life of Charles Dickens*, ed. J. W. T. Ley (1928) · *The letters of Charles Dickens*, ed. M. House, G. Storey, and others, 12 vols. (1965–2002), 1–12 · R. Langton, *The childhood and youth of Charles Dickens* (1891) · *The speeches of Charles Dickens*, ed. K. J. Fielding (1960) · *Dickens's journalism*, ed. M. Slater and J. Drew, Dent Uniform Edition, 1–4 (1994–2000) · M. Allen, *Charles Dickens's childhood* (1988) · F. G. Kitton, ed., *Charles Dickens by pen and pencil* (1890) · R. L. Patten, *Dickens and his publishers* (1978) · E. Johnson, *Charles Dickens: his tragedy and triumph*, 2 vols. (1952) · P. Ackroyd, *Dickens* (1990) · P. Schlicke, ed., *Oxford reader's companion to Dickens* (1999) · M. Slater, *Dickens and women* (1983) · P. Collins, ed., *Dickens: the critical heritage* (1971) · P. Collins, ed., *Dickens: interviews and recollections*, 2 vols. (1981) · K. Perugini, ' "Edwin Drood" and the last days of Charles Dickens', *Pall Mall Magazine*, 37 (June 1906), 643–52 · G. Storey, *Dickens and daughter* (1939) · M. Dickens, *My father as I recall him* (1896) · G. Dolby, *Charles Dickens as I knew him* (1885) · G. Curry, *Dickens and Annie Fields* (1988) · P. Collins, ed., *Charles Dickens: the public readings* (1975) · C. Tomalin, *The invisible woman: the story of Nelly Ternan and Charles Dickens*, new edn (1991) · *Shaw on Dickens*, ed. D. Laurence and M. Quinn (1985) · G. Ford, *Dickens and his readers* (1955) · P. Bolton, *Dickens dramatised* (1987) · J. Cohen, *Charles Dickens and his original illustrators* (1980) · K. Chittick, *Dickens in the 1830s* (1990) · D. Walder, *Dickens and religion* (1981) · N. Pope, *Dickens and charity* (1978)

# *Index*

# Enjoy biography? Explore more than 55,000 life stories in the Oxford Dictionary of National Biography

The biographies in the 'Very Interesting People' series derive from the *Oxford Dictionary of National Biography*—available in 60 print volumes and online.

To find out about the lives of more than 55,000 people who shaped all aspects of Britain's past worldwide, visit the *Oxford DNB* website at **www.oxforddnb.com**.

## There's lots to discover ...

Read about remarkable people in all walks of life—not just the great and good, but those who left a mark, be they good, bad, or bizarre.

Browse through more than 10,000 portrait illustrations— the largest selection of national portraiture ever published.

Regular features on history in the news—with links to biographies—provide fascinating insights into topical events.

## Get a life ... by email

Why not sign up to receive the free *Oxford DNB* 'Life of the Day' by email? Entertaining, informative, and topical biographies delivered direct to your inbox—a great way to start the day.

## Find out more at www.oxforddnb.com

*'An intellectual wonderland for all scholars and enthusiasts'*

Tristram Hunt, *The Times*

### *The finest scholarship on the greatest people...*

Many leading biographers and scholars have contributed articles on the most influential figures in British history: for example, Paul Addison on Winston Churchill, Patrick Collinson on Elizabeth I, Lyndall Gordon on Virginia Woolf, Christopher Ricks on Alfred Tennyson, Frank Barlow on Thomas Becket, Fiona MacCarthy on William Morris, Roy Jenkins on Harold Wilson.

*'Paul Addison's Churchill ... is a miniature masterpiece.'*

Piers Brendon, *The Independent*

### *Every story fascinates...*

The *Oxford DNB* contains stories of courage, malice, romance, dedication, ambition, and comedy, capturing the diversity and delights of human conduct. Discover the Irish bishop who was also an accomplished boomerang thrower, the historian who insisted on having 'Not Yours' inscribed on the inside of his hats, and the story of the philanthropist and friend of Dickens Angela Burdett-Coutts, who defied convention by proposing to the Duke of Wellington when he was seventy-seven and she was just thirty. He turned her down.

*'Every story fascinates. The new ODNB will enrich your life, and the national life.'*

Matthew Parris, *The Spectator*

**www.oxforddnb.com**

At 60,000 pages in 60 volumes, the *Oxford Dictionary of National Biography* is one of the largest single works ever printed in English.

The award-winning online edition of the *Oxford DNB* makes it easy to explore the dictionary with great speed and ease. It also provides regular updates of new lives and topical features.

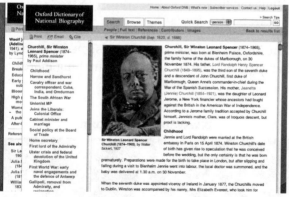

# www.oxforddnb.com

The *Oxford Dictionary of National Biography* was created in partnership with the British Academy by scholars of international standing.

It was edited by the late Professor H. C. G. Matthew, Professor of Modern History, University of Oxford, and Professor Sir Brian Harrison, Professor of Modern History, University of Oxford, with the assistance of 14 consultant editors and 470 associate editors worldwide.

Dr Lawrence Goldman, Fellow and Tutor in Modern History, St Peter's College, Oxford, became editor in October 2004.

### *What readers say*

'The *Oxford DNB* is a major work of reference, but it also contains some of the best gossip in the world.'

John Gross, *Sunday Telegraph*

'A fine genealogical research tool that allows you to explore family history, heredity, and even ethnic identity.'

Margaret Drabble, *Prospect*

'The huge website is superbly designed and easy to navigate. Who could ask for anything more?'

Humphrey Carpenter, *Sunday Times*

## **www.oxforddnb.com**